THE NEW OXFORD PICTURE DICTIONARY

Intermediate Workbook

by
JILL WAGNER SCHIMPFF

D0573071

Oxford University Press
1988

Oxford University Press

200 Madison Avenue
New York, NY 10016 USA

Walton Street
Oxford OX2 6DP England

OXFORD is a trademark of Oxford University Press.
ISBN 0-19-434325-1

Senior Editor: Margot Gramer
Associate Editor: Mary Lynne Nielsen
Designer: Maj-Britt Hagsted

Printing (last digit): 10 9 8 7 6 5 4 3

Printed in the United States of America.

To Warren and the computer he convinced me to get!

Contents

To the Teacher

The *Intermediate Workbook* has been specifically designed to accompany *The New Oxford Picture Dictionary.* It is suitable for students of English as a Second Language at low through high-intermediate levels.

The main purpose of the *Workbook* is to provide practice with and reinforcement of the Dictionary vocabulary. Naturally, the teacher should introduce and clarify the vocabulary before related *Workbook* pages are attempted.

A variety of uses can be made of individual exercises. For example, a fill-in-the-blank exercise may stress vocabulary retention, but it may also be a good reading exercise or a good lesson on the use of articles. Many of the exercises in the *Workbook* are also valuable for stimulating discussion.

The units of the *Workbook* are organized sequentially; however, the units do not need to be taught in their specific order. For this reason, bold numbers in the exercise instructions indicate that vocabulary from a previous Dictionary page is being reviewed.

Each exercise is marked for level of difficulty to help teachers select exercises suited to the particular needs of their students. The key at the bottom of the page explains this coding. Blue ink is used to indicate sample answers throughout the *Workbook.* This convention should be explained to the students initially and thereafter it should be evident to them.

Key

 low-intermediate exercise

intermediate exercise

high-intermediate exercise

THE NEW OXFORD PICTURE DICTIONARY

Intermediate Workbook

1 Groups

Look at all of the words on pages 2–3. On another sheet of paper, divide them into three groups—one group for males, another for females, and the third for those who can be either male or female.

2 A Family Survey

Answer these questions about your family.

1. Do you have a husband or wife? _____

   Do you have any children? _____

   How many daughters? _____

   Sons? _____

2. How many children do your parents have?
   (Remember to count yourself!) _____

3. How many older sisters do you have? _____

   Younger sisters? _____

   Older brothers? _____

   Younger brothers? _____

4. How many brothers-in-law do you have? _____

5. How many sisters-in-law do you have? _____

6. How many nieces do you have? _____

   Nephews? _____

7. Do you have any nieces or nephews who are older than you? _____

8. How many grandchildren do your grandparents have? _____

   Mother's parents? _____

   Father's parents? _____

9. How many children do most families in your country have? _____

10. Do you ever have big family reunions? _____

    How often? _____

    Where? _____

3 It's for You!

Read the conversations and decide whom the speaker wants to talk to.

> A: Hi! Is the birthday girl there? I want to wish her a happy 75th birthday.
>
> B: I'll get her, John.

1. He wants to talk to his   1. grandfather.   2. grandmother.   3. uncle.

A: Hi, sweetie. Is Mom there?   B: She's right here, Dad.

2. He wants to talk to his   1. niece.   2. daughter.   3. wife.

A: Hello, this is Uncle Fred speaking. Is Alice home?   B: Sure, I'll tell her that her favorite uncle wants her!

3. He wants to talk to his   1. sister-in-law.   2. aunt.   3. niece.

A: This is your Aunt Elsie. Is your brother Bob there?   B: No, but I'll tell him you called.

4. She wants to talk to her   1. sister-in-law.   2. cousin.   3. nephew.

A: Hi, big sister. Is your husband home?   B: He's right here, Nancy.

5. She wants to talk to her   1. cousin.   2. brother-in-law.   3. uncle.

A: Hello, honey. Is your brother there?   B: Just a minute, I'll see, Grandma.

6. She wants to talk to her   1. granddaughter.   2. grandson.   3. father.

A: Hi, Marty. Is your dad close by?   B: Wait a second, Grandpa. He's in the garage.

7. He wants to talk to his   1. son.   2. brother.   3. nephew.

4 A Favorite Relative

1. Choose a favorite male relative and write two or three sentences about him on another sheet of paper.

2. Do the same thing for a female relative.

3. Write about a young boy in your family.

4. Do the same thing for a young girl in your family.

2 The Human Body pages 4–5

1 Odd Man Out

● Circle the word that doesn't belong. Tell why on the line below.
○○

1. knee   thigh   (back)   calf

   It's not part of the leg.

2. hip   shoulder   buttocks   abdomen

   _____

3. abdomen   forearm   elbow   knuckle

   _____

4. neck   throat   instep   chin

   _____

5. face   knuckle   fingernail   palm

   _____

2 Head, Eye, and Internal Organs

● Read the definitions below and write a good answer.
○○ There may be more than one answer.

1. This is used for eating. _____

2. This is over the eye. _____

3. This is a black circle in the eye. _____

4. This is used to smell. _____

5. These are used for hard work. _____

6. This is hair on a man's face. _____

7. This is used to think. _____

8. These are hairs on the eyelid. _____

9. This is hair over the top lip. _____

10. This is the colored part of the eye. ____

11. This carries blood to the heart. _____

12. This is pink and is used to talk. _____

3 Crazy Words

Find a crazy word in all but one of the following sentences. Circle the one sentence that makes sense. Cross out the crazy word in the rest of the sentences and write a better word on the line.

1. She put the ring on her ~~thumb~~. *ring finger*

2. It hurts to swallow—she has a sore arm. _____

3. The pain went from her elbow through her thigh to her shoulder. _____

4. Her hair was so long it fell to her heels. _____

5. He broke his armpit while running. _____

6. He must have a cold in his ear because he is coughing. _____

7. She hit the dog with the palm of her hand. _____

8. She wore bright red nail polish on her chin. _____

9. He broke his knuckle when he kicked the rock. _____

10. Her shoes were too small and hurt her calf. _____

4 Overheard Conversations

What parts of the body are the following conversations about? There may be more than one good answer.

Beauty Parlor
A: How do you like the way it looks?
B: It's wonderful. You look great as a blonde! _____

Hospital
A: You need to keep off it for a week.
B: Thanks, the crutches will help. _____

Barber Shop
A: Shall I cut them so they're even with the bottom of your ears?
B: No, leave them a little bit shorter than that. _____

Doctor's Office
A: I have to try to relax more.
B: Right. You may not be as lucky if you have another attack. _____

3 Vegetables pages 6–7

1 Buying

Choose several vegetables. How can you buy them? Place a
check mark under the appropriate columns.

	BY THE DOZEN	CANNED	BUNCH	ONE BY ONE	BY THE POUND
1. _____					
2. _____					
3. _____					
4. _____					
5. _____					

2 Supermarket Ads

Choose a vegetable to go with each ad and write it on the line
below. There may be more than one good answer.

sweet, not strong will not make you cry!	Cheaper by the 10 lb. bag!	CRISP & LEAFY GREAT for SALAD!
1. _____	2. _____	3. _____

Three beautiful white heads for only $1.00	RED, RIPE, JUICY!	buy 12 and get 1 ear free!
4. _____	5. _____	6. _____

5

TWO STALKS for 89¢	*Tender pods—* *Great for stir fry!*	**3 cloves for only 49¢**

7. _____ 8. _____ 9. _____

3   A Shopping List

Make a list of vegetables to buy in order to make the following
dishes. You may use a vegetable more than once.

vegetable soup   **green salad**

_____   _____

_____   _____

_____   _____

_____   _____

potato salad   **coleslaw**

_____   _____

_____   _____

_____   _____

_____   _____

pizza   **stir fry**

_____   _____

_____   _____

_____   _____

_____   _____

6

4 Survey

Answer the following questions with complete sentences.

1. Name five of your favorite vegetables. _____

    _____

    Why do you like them? _____

2. Which vegetables do you hate? _____

    _____

    Why? _____

3. Which of the vegetables in the Dictionary are most common in your

    home country? _____

    _____

    What are some vegetables that are <u>not</u> in the Dictionary and are hard

    to find here? _____

    _____

4. What vegetables do you like to eat raw? _____

    _____

5 A Favorite Dish

On another sheet of paper, explain how you would fix your
favorite vegetable dish. Give the approximate recipe and
describe how to put it together. If you're not a cook, simply
describe your favorite vegetable dish.

4 Fruits pages 8–9

1 The Pick of the Crop

● Each of these states is famous for the pictured fruit. Look at the
○○ fruit in the Dictionary and finish the sentences for pictures 1–4.
Decide how to write sentences 5–10.

Washington

1. Washington is famous for _____

Michigan

2. _____ come from _____

Georgia

3. _____ grow well in _____

Hawaii

4. _____ grows wonderful _____

California

5. _____

Florida

6. _____

Maine

7. _____

Georgia

8. _____

Oregon

9. _____

Texas

10. _____

8

2 What Is It?

Find as many answers as possible for each statement. Your answers may be different from your neighbor's.

1. You can get "milk" from this. _____

2. These are always sour. _____

3. Monkeys like these. _____

4. You can make good juice from these. _____

5. You can find them in candy bars. _____

6. You can make wine from these. _____

7. You often sprinkle salt on these. _____

8. You can eat these with a spoon. _____

9. You crack these open with a knife. _____

10. You often sprinkle sugar on these. _____

3 Fruit Salad

The following recipe for fruit salad is not given correctly. Put the lines into the correct order by numbering 1,2,3, etc. The first one is done.

_____ some walnuts on top and serve.

_____ leaves into small pieces. Mix all of the

_____ grapes and strawberries into halves. Make

_____ fruit salad onto the six lettuce leaves. Put

_____ lemon juice, and two tablespoons of orange juice.

_____ peel an orange and section it. Tear six lettuce

_____ above fruit in a large salad bowl. Spoon some of the

___1___ Peel and slice the peaches and bananas. Cut the

_____ a dressing with a mixture of ³/₄ cup honey, two tablespoons of

_____ Prepare the pineapple chunks and slice the pears. Next,

4 Idioms

Here are some common expressions using fruit. Work with several other students to see if you can find out what each one means. Do you think they are nice things to say or not? Put a plus (+) or a minus (−) after each expression to show whether it's a positive or negative thing to say. Write a short definition.

1. the apple of my eye _____

_____

2. the top banana _____

_____

3. a peach _____

_____

4. a plum _____

_____

5. a lemon _____

_____

6. a nut _____

_____

1 Likes and Dislikes

Look at the following chart carefully. Then decide whether the following sentences are true (T), false (F), or impossible to know (?).

Family Tastes

	Mrs. Smith	Mr. Smith	Tim	Sally	Grandma	Grandpa

1. Sally likes lobster. _____
2. Mrs. Smith dislikes clams. _____
3. Tim doesn't like crab. _____
4. Mrs. Smith likes bacon. _____
5. Sally hates ham. _____

6. Grandpa dislikes ground beef. _____
7. Grandma loves mussels. _____
8. Mr. Smith likes chicken. _____
9. Tim likes lamb chops. _____
10. Grandma doesn't like oysters. _____

2 Your Family Tastes

Make a chart with six of your family members' names. Write in what they like and dislike. Then write sentences that say what they like and dislike.

3 My Favorite Foods

Make a list of your own favorite and least favorite foods. Then form sentences like the examples. Do the same for your family members.

I like chicken, but I don't like ham.
My brother likes fish, but he doesn't like oysters.

1 Packaging

Look at the picture in the Dictionary and decide what foods come in what containers. Then complete these sentences.

eggs   1. I bought *a carton of eggs*.

gum   2. _____ in her purse.

tuna   3. I opened _____

soap   4. _____ to wash my hands.

cookies   5. _____ cost $1.69.

margarine   6. _____ in the refrigerator.

crackers   7. _____ on the shelf.

butter   8. I unwrapped _____

oil   9. _____ on the table.

soda   10. We drank _____

potato chips 11. Where is _____

hair spray   12. _____ in the bathroom.

toothpaste   13. I squeezed _____

bread   14. I don't need _____

stamps   15. _____ at the post office.

toilet paper 16. He bought 12 _____

mayonnaise   17. _____ large _____

yogurt   18. Did you buy _____

liquid soap   19. I can't find _____

2 Continue on Your Own

Go back to exercise 1. Choose another kind of food and write a sentence for that type of container. For example: *I opened a carton of milk.*

3 It All Adds Up

Read each sentence to find out how much money each person has.

1. Ted has three quarters, a dime, and a nickel.   *Ted has $ .90.*

2. Marcia has three dimes, two nickels, and two pennies. _____

3. Together, Cindy and Tom have one five-dollar bill,
   one one-dollar bill, a quarter, and six pennies. _____

4. Mrs. Garcia has three one-dollar bills,
   four quarters, one dime, and one penny. _____

4 It's All the Same to Me

Different combinations of bills and coins may add up to the
same total. For each given amount, write out three possible
combinations. Complete the exercise on another sheet of paper.

1. $1.97 a. *one one-dollar bill, three quarters, two dimes, two pennies*
        b. *six quarters, four dimes, one nickel, two pennies*
        c. *one one-dollar bill, two quarters, four dimes, one nickel, two pennies*

2. $ .49   3. $3.52   4. $7.68   5. $14.23   6. $21.16

5 The Correct Change, Please!

Read each situation. Give the customer the correct change.
(There is more than one way.) Write your answers on another sheet of paper.

1. Sue Cory bought groceries for $36.42. She gave the clerk four
   ten-dollar bills. Her change?
   $3.58. Three one-dollar bills, two quarters, one nickel, and three pennies.

2. Bill Ryan got a new TV for $157.50. He gave the clerk two
   hundred-dollar bills. His change?

3. Marilyn Monson bought a candy bar for 39¢. She only had a
   ten-dollar bill. Her change?

4. George Gately got a new shirt for $22.39. He gave the clerk a
   fifty-dollar bill. His change?

5. When Betty Butterworth bought her groceries, she made a check
   out for more than the amount she owed so that she would have
   cash. The groceries cost $67.94. She wrote this on the check:
   Seventy-five and 00/100 dollars. Her change?

1 At the Market

Fill in the blanks with the best words. There may be more than one correct answer. You may use an answer more than once.

1. Find the frozen foods in the _____.

2. You'll find the bread in _____ one.

3. Put your groceries in a _____.

4. Early in the morning there often aren't many _____ in the supermarket.

5. We weighed the _____ on _____.

6. I found the _____ in a bin.

7. The _____ were on the _____.

8. The cashier handed him his _____.

9. I had to show my check cashing card to cash my _____.

10. The _____ showed how much change I should get.

2 A Mix-Up

Put the following sentences into logical order. The first sentence is already marked.

_____ I paid with a check.

_____ I waited in line at the checkout counter.

_____ The cashier rang up my groceries on the cash register.

___1___ Yesterday I went shopping at the supermarket.

_____ The cashier gave me my change.

_____ When I was next, I took my groceries out of my cart and put them on the conveyor belt.

_____ I pushed my shopping cart up and down the aisles.

3 Check Out the Supermarket!

Look at the picture. All of the following statements about it are wrong. Read each one carefully and correct them on another sheet of paper. There may be several ways to correct the sentences.

1. There are 15 shopping carts in the picture.

2. Three shoppers have shopping baskets.

3. A woman is paying cash for her groceries.

4. There is only one person working at the deli counter.

5. There is a receipt hanging over the produce section.

6. The freezer section has four doors.

7. The older woman shopper at the checkout counter has a full shopping cart of groceries.

8. There is a check coming out of the top of one of the cash registers.

9. One of the shoppers with a shopping basket is choosing a carton of milk.

10. The deli counter is near the checkout counters.

4 My Supermarket

Look at the picture. Does the supermarket where you shop look like this? On another sheet of paper, tell how your supermarket is different.

1 Strip Stories

Look at the following strip stories. On the lines below, write the words from page 16 that you see.

A.

_____ _____ _____ _____

B.

_____ _____ _____ _____

C.

_____ _____ _____ _____

2 Action in Writing

Write a sentence describing each picture of the stories in exercise 1. Study the example.

A. 1. *A waiter is serving a couple sandwiches and drinks.*

3 My Favorite Place

On another sheet of paper, describe your favorite restaurant in the United States. Tell why you like to go there, when you usually go, and what you like to order. Is it an expensive place?

1 Verbs/People Match

Look at the verbs on page 17. Match the following people with the verbs. You may use a verb more than once.

Bartender _____

Waiter _____

Customer _____

Cook _____

Busboy _____

Cocktail Waitress _____

2 Sentence Part Match

Match the sentence beginnings to the sentence endings. There should be one match for each. Review page **16** before you begin.

___h___ 1. The waiter is holding

_____ 2. The waitress is giving

_____ 3. The cook is burning

_____ 4. The girl is drinking

_____ 5. The customer is lighting

_____ 6. The customer is eating

_____ 7. The bartender is taking

_____ 8. The customer is paying

_____ 9. The busboy is clearing

_____ 10. The cocktail waitress is holding

a. the beer from the tap.

b. the menu to the customer.

c. the table with a tray.

d. his sandwich in the booth.

e. her soft drink from a straw.

f. our food in the kitchen.

g. her cigarette with a lighter.

h. the tray over his head.

i. the wine bottle in her hand.

j. the check at the cash register.

3 Do-It-Yourself Project

Look at the sentence beginnings in exercise 2. On another sheet of paper, add your own endings to the sentences.

4 Cause and Result

For each action, give a logical result.

1. After the waiter serves the food, *the customer eats the food.*

2. After the busboy clears the table, _____

3. After the waitress gives the check to the customer, _____

4. After the waiter gives the menu to the customer, _____

5. After the bartender serves the drinks, _____

6. After the cook cooks the food, _____

5 Restaurant Jobs

Write the answers to these questions on another sheet of paper.
Report to the class.

1. Have you ever worked in a restaurant? If so, where? When?
    What type of job? What was the name of the restaurant?

2. Think of all of the people who work in a restaurant. For each of
    the jobs, mention at least two advantages and two
    disadvantages.

18

10 Common Prepared Foods page 18

1 Roleplay

Choose six students from the class to play the people in the chart. Choose a waiter/waitress, and roleplay the orders.

Jill	Danny	Dave	Peggy	Sally	Jim

2 Model Sentences

On another sheet of paper, make as many sentences as you can using at least one word from each of the three groups. Study the examples.

PEOPLE		VERBS			FOODS AND ITEMS	
waitress	waiter	spread	eat	set	tray	sandwiches
busboy	customer	order	hold	clear	biscuit	soft drinks
cook	bartender	serve	buy	cook	beer	beef stew
cocktail waitress		pay	drink	take	food	table
		give			toast	mustard
					check	bottle of wine
					eggs	

The customer is eating toast.   *The waitress will serve the eggs.*   *I told the busboy to clear the table.*

3 Tasty Combinations

The following foods are usually eaten with something else. For each word, write a sentence telling what other food you would eat with it. There are many possible answers. Look at the examples.

1. ketchup *I like ketchup on my hamburgers.*

    I put ketchup on my french fries.

    Ketchup is good on steak.

2. biscuits _____

3. mustard _____

4. butter _____

5. bacon _____

6. jelly _____

7. roll _____

8. potato chips _____

9. pickle _____

10. salad dressing _____

11. bun _____

12. coffee _____

13. syrup _____

4 Desserts

Complete these sentences in interesting ways. Don't repeat!

1. This sundae _____

2. Sundaes are _____

3. _____ sundaes.

4. This ice cream cone _____

20

5. Ice cream cones are _____

6. _____ ice cream cones.

7. This cookie _____

8. Cookies are _____

9. _____ cookies.

10. This strawberry shortcake is _____

11. Strawberry shortcakes are _____

12. _____ strawberry shortcake.

5 Food Survey

Choose a partner and ask each other the following questions.
Report your findings to the class.

1. Which foods on page 18 are for breakfast? Lunch? Dinner?

_____

2. What is a typical breakfast in your native country? Lunch? Dinner?

_____

3. What are a few favorite desserts in your native country?

_____

4. At what time do you eat breakfast at home? Lunch? Dinner?

_____

5. Here in the United States, how often do you eat out?

_____

6. How often do you get takeout food to bring home? What kind?

_____

7. What is fast food? How often do you eat it?

_____

6 The Yum Yum Restaurant

Look at the picture and fill in the blanks with any sensible words from pages **16, 17,** or **18.** You may use a word more than once.

Steve Taylor goes to the Yum Yum Restaurant every day. His brother-in-law owns it, and it is the

worst restaurant in town! For example, the _____ always burns the

_____ . The _____ often drops the _____ . If someone

orders a hamburger, he always has to ask the _____ for the _____ .

Steve's _____ never comes the way he likes it, either. One time Steve ordered

_____ , but the _____ served him _____ ! There is never

any _____ or _____ on the table. The toast comes without

_____ , and the _____ is never hot. What is even worse, the

_____ are always greasy and the _____ are always cold. There is never

a _____ _____ for Steve's little boy, nor is there an _____

on the table for Steve, who smokes. When he got up to _____ the

_____ the _____ gave him the wrong change! Steve has to talk to his

brother-in-law!

11 Outdoor Clothes page 19

1 Which Is Warmer?

Which clothes are warmer in your opinion? Write your answers on another sheet of paper.

1. beret/ski cap

   A ski cap is warmer.

2. crewneck sweater/V-neck sweater

3. rain boots/hiking boots

4. windbreaker/coat

5. mittens/gloves

6. blue jeans/tights

7. jacket/parka

8. earmuffs/cap

9. flannel shirt/coat

2 But I Didn't Think It Would . . . .

Often we forget to wear the correct clothes outside. See if you can find out what each person below forgot. Read each situation and describe what the person needs.

1. My hands are cold! *You need gloves.*

2. It's too bad we can't skate on that beautiful ice! _____

3. The wind is cold on my neck! _____

4. My ears are cold! _____

5. I can't feel my feet. _____

6. I'm cold all over. _____

7. It's hard to carry all the extra clothes! _____

8. Oh no, it's raining! _____

9. My head is freezing. _____

10. It's too bad we can't hike into the mountains! _____

3 Clothes and Climate

In some climates, lots of outdoor clothes are necessary. In others, almost none are needed. Write about how much outdoor clothing is needed in your part of the world. Which of the clothes on page 19 are most commonly used in your native country, and which are never used?

12 Everyday Clothes pages 20–21

1 Help!

●
○○ Look at the following pictures and decide what items would help each person. Study the example.

1. *He should get a belt.*

5. _____

2. _____

6. _____

3. _____

7. _____

4. _____

8. _____

2 What's the Difference?

Look at the pictures and tell what makes the clothes different.
Follow the example.

A.    B.    1. *B doesn't have high heels.*

A.    B.    2. _____

A.    B.   3. _____

A.    B.    4. _____

A.    B.    5. _____

A.    B.    6. _____

3 Going to Work

Look at the picture in the Dictionary and describe what each
person is wearing. You could begin your paragraph with these
sentences:

*It's early in the morning, and there's a long line of people waiting for the
bus. The first person in line is wearing a maroon uniform, black shoes, black
tie, and a cap.*

1 Inseparables

Look at the words below. Find another word that is often worn with the given word. Write sentences about these pairs.

1. undershirts   *Undershirts go with boxer shorts.*

2. garter belts _____

3. pajamas _____

4. panties _____

5. girdles _____

6. nightgowns _____

7. socks _____

2 Over and Under

Most underwear is worn under other items of clothing. Complete the sentences below.

1. A half slip is worn under *a skirt*.

2. A half slip is worn over *pantyhose*.

3. A bra is worn under _____ .

4. Men's slacks are worn over _____ .

5. Undershirts are worn under _____ .

6. A full slip is worn under _____ .

7. A man's suit jacket is worn over _____ , which is worn over _____ .

3 Dictionary Definitions

Read the definition and give the word that matches it. You may have to look up some of the definition words in a larger dictionary.

1. a short, sleeveless undergarment for women _____

2. a woman's tight-fitting undergarment that goes from the waist to below the hips _____

3. a light, low-cut shoe that is easily slipped on _____

4. full-length underwear worn for warmth _____

5. two-piece, lightweight suit designed for sleeping _____

6. short, tight-fitting underpants for men _____

7. loose-fitting men's underpants _____

8. long, loose women's sleepwear _____

9. knitted coverings for the feet that go above the ankle _____

10. a woman's undergarment, of dress length, with straps _____

4 Times Have Changed

Underwear styles have changed a lot since our grandparents' days. Write about how the underwear you wear is different from what your grandmother or grandfather wore. Start with this — *In my grandparents' day, underwear styles were very different.*

1   Getting Ready

Make a list on another sheet of paper of all the possible toiletries and makeup that might be needed in the following situations.

1. Jane looked in the mirror to make up her eyes.

2. Rob had a 7 p.m. appointment, so he decided to shave a second time.

3. On her lunch break Doris clipped, filed, and polished her nails.

4. Sara made up her lips and cheeks before she went to the party.

2   Dialogues in a Jewelry/Cosmetics Department

Read the conversations and decide what jewelry or cosmetics the people are talking about.

1.
Clerk: Do you want silver or gold?
Woman: The gold one is better. It's longer. I don't like them too tight around my neck.

_____

2.
Clerk: Does she have pierced ears?
Man: No, she doesn't.
Clerk: Then these would be better.

_____

3.
Clerk: Do you like the one with the black or the brown band best?
Man: I don't care. Which one tells the time best?

_____

4.
Man: The diamond one is beautiful. I'm going to ask her to marry me tonight!
Clerk: Congratulations!

_____

5.
Woman: This one is too loose.
Clerk: Yes, you have very thin wrists.

_____

6.
Woman: My husband will like the gold one.
Clerk: Does he wear clips or pins?
Woman: A clip is best.

_____

3   On Your Own

Write a short paragraph about perfume or after-shave lotion. Do you like to wear it? If so, what kind? If not, why not? Mention if you like members of the opposite sex to wear it.

15 Describing Clothes page 24

1 Short Stories

● Fill in the blanks of the stories below the pictures. Use words
○○ from page 24.

Jerry Davis is on his way to the office. Today

he has on a _____-sleeved shirt with

a _____, _____ vest. He

hates ties, so his _____,

_____ tie is _____ around his

neck. Jerry doesn't see that his briefcase is

_____.

Betty Sargent is a clerk in a department store.

She has on a _____-sleeved

_____ blouse, a _____ skirt,

and _____, _____-heeled

shoes. She is showing a customer a

_____ purse.

2 Likes

● Use an adjective to describe your favorite kind of each item
●○ below. Write your sentences on another sheet of paper.

1. ties
   Striped ties are my favorites.
   I like striped ties best.
   Striped ties look best on me!

2. shirts	5. slacks	8. sneakers	11. dresses
3. shoes	6. jackets	9. shorts	12. hats
4. purses	7. blazers	10. T-shirts	13. sandals

29

3 And Dislikes

Now, using the words in exercise 2, describe the kind of each item that you hate the most. Look at the examples.

I hate plaid ties the most.
Plaid ties are my least favorites.

4 Classroom Fashion

Use the words on pages **20–21** and page 24 to describe, on another sheet of paper, what you are wearing today. Then write a complete description of what one of your classmates is wearing. Read your descriptions to the class to see if anyone can guess who the people are!

16 Describing the Weather page 25

1 The Weather Forecast

Look at the following weather map and the key below it. Read the forecast and fill in the blanks with appropriate words. You may use a word more than once.

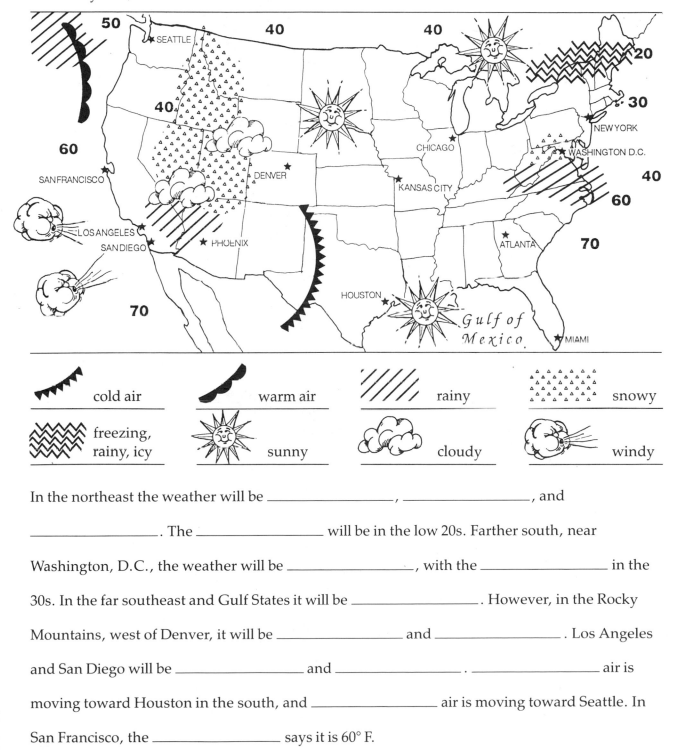

cold air	warm air	rainy	snowy
freezing, rainy, icy	sunny	cloudy	windy

In the northeast the weather will be _____, _____, and

_____. The _____ will be in the low 20s. Farther south, near

Washington, D.C., the weather will be _____, with the _____ in the

30s. In the far southeast and Gulf States it will be _____. However, in the Rocky

Mountains, west of Denver, it will be _____ and _____. Los Angeles

and San Diego will be _____ and _____. _____ air is

moving toward Houston in the south, and _____ air is moving toward Seattle. In

San Francisco, the _____ says it is 60° F.

31

2 The Perfect Day?

Tell what kind of day it probably is based on the sentences below. There may be more than one good answer.

1. Watch out for sunburn.   *It must be sunny.*

2. Don't step in any puddles of water!   _____

3. You can't see ten feet in front of you!   _____

4. Walk carefully so you don't slip.   _____

5. Leave your sweater at home today.   _____

6. It's a good day for an ice cream cone.   _____

7. Wear a sweater.   _____

8. Wear your rain boots.   _____

9. Wear your snow boots.   _____

10. Wear your windbreaker.   _____

3 World Climate

In four paragraphs, describe what the climate is like in your native country. Include all four seasons: winter, spring, summer, and fall. Your teacher might like to read these to the class to see if any students can guess what part of the world is being described.

17 Seasonal Verbs page 26
Houses page 27

1 Riddles

Find the answers to these riddles on page 27. Write complete sentences for the answers. There may be more than one good answer.

1. It cooks food and sounds like will.

   A grill cooks food.

2. Wear this when you cook.

3. Use this to gather leaves.

4. Burn these on a grill.

5. Drive up this.

6. Rest on this.

7. This keeps out flies.

8. This cuts wood very quickly.

9. Open this on a hot day.

10. Use this when you dig deep holes.

11. Put leaves in this.

12. Put your car here.

13. Smoke comes out of this.

14. Water your garden with this.

15. Wear these to protect your hands.

16. Use this to turn hamburgers.

2 Put It All Together

Find the best endings for these beginnings.

_____ 1. She has to paint

_____ 2. Try to push the heavy

_____ 3. Because of the snow, you should sand

_____ 4. The roses are dry, so I'm looking for

_____ 5. They want to clean

_____ 6. They have to wear

_____ 7. We like to lie

_____ 8. The whole family is sitting

a. the watering can.

b. work gloves.

c. the dirty windows.

d. on the porch.

e. wheelbarrow.

f. the driveway.

g. in the hammock.

h. the gutter.

3 What Should They Do?

Read each situation below and, on another sheet of paper, write what the people should do.

1. It's spring, and there's a lot of tall grass in Mr. Smith's backyard.

   He should mow the grass with the lawn mower.

2. It's winter, and there is a lot of snow in front of Jane White's house.

3. It's spring, and there are no flowers in Jason Brand's backyard.

4. It's fall, and there are lots of leaves in Betty Jackson's backyard.

5. It's summer, and Mr. Jones's flowers are dry.

6. It's winter, and Donna Scott's driveway is icy.

7. It's spring, and Danny Myer's hedge is too high.

4 It Can't Be True!

The following sentences are all false. Look at the picture on page 27 and correct the sentences. There may be many good answers.

1. There's a wheelbarrow on the roof.
   There's a chimney on the roof.
   There's a wheelbarrow in the toolshed.

2. The driveway is next to the TV antenna.

_____

3. The toolshed is in the garage.

_____

4. The lawn mower is on the lounge chair.

_____

5. The shovel is in the grill.

_____

6. The mitt and spatula are next to the watering can.

_____

5 Useless Items!

Choose several items from page 26 that would not be useful at a house in your native country. Write a short paragraph telling why you wouldn't need these items.

1 Good Advice

Match the following problems and advice.

_____ 1. The fireplace is empty!

_____ 2. Where can I study?

_____ 3. I'm tired!

_____ 4. It's too sunny in here!

_____ 5. I'm hot!

_____ 6. I'm cold!

_____ 7. It's so dark in here!

_____ 8. There's nothing to do!

_____ 9. Where can I put my coffee?

a. Turn on the lamp.

b. Turn on the ceiling fan.

c. Watch TV for a while.

d. Lie down on the sofa.

e. Get some logs.

f. Set it on the coffee table.

g. Use the desk.

h. Stand next to the fire.

i. Pull the drapes.

2 The Sunnydale Survey

Look at the bar graph. These are the results of a survey describing what's in the living rooms of 100 people in Sunnydale, USA. Write a paragraph describing the results.

All of the homes in Sunnydale have TVs in the living room.

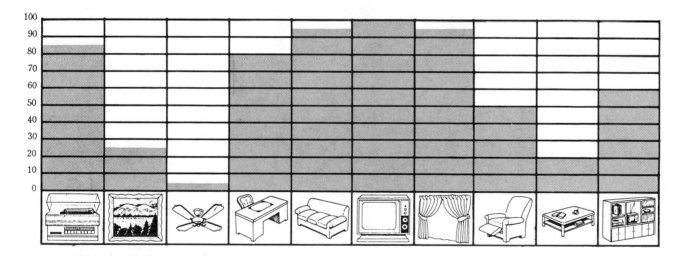

3 A Group Survey

Get together with four other students. Survey the group, and then make a graph for your group like the one above. Write the names of the pieces of furniture at the bottom of each column.

19 The Dining Room page 29

1 Picture Puzzle

Look at the picture in the Dictionary carefully. Then answer these questions on the lines provided.

1. What's burning on the buffet? *The candles are.*

2. What's next to the water glass? _____

3. What covers the table? _____

4. What's the large bowl on the buffet? _____

5. What's on the plates? _____

6. Where are the coffee pot and teapot? _____

7. What has its doors open? _____

8. What's in the open drawer? _____

9. What stands at the end of the table? _____

10. What does the man have in his right hand? _____

11. What does the woman have in her hand? _____

2 Now You Do It!

Write five questions of your own based on the picture. Have another student answer them.

1. _____

2. _____

3. _____

4. _____

5. _____

3 The Dinner

Make up sentences to complete these dinner dialogues. Use as many words from page 29 as possible in each one.

1.

Guest: May I pour the water?

Host: *Sure. The water pitcher is on the buffet.*

Guest: OK, I see it.

2.

Hostess: _____

Guest: No, thanks, I don't put anything in my coffee.

Hostess: _____

Guest: No, thanks, the food tastes fine just as it is.

3.

Guest: Tell me where the silverware and china is. I'd like to help you set the table.

Hostess: _____

Guest: OK, and where do I put the knife, fork, spoon, and napkin? We do it a little differently in my country.

Hostess: _____

Guest: And what about the water glass, wine glass, and bread plate? Where do they go?

Hostess: _____

Guest: Thanks, it's good to know the customs.

4.

Guest: I hope you'll enjoy these flowers!

Hostess: _____

Guest: Yes, they'll look very pretty there.

20 The Kitchen page 30

1 Kitchen Duty

●
○○ Make a list of all the possible utensils, dishes, pots, pans, and appliances that would be needed in the following situations.

1. Pete got up and made a breakfast of toast and coffee.

_____

2. Karen opened a bottle of soda and then filled her glass with ice cubes.

_____

3. Steve washed and dried the dishes by hand and then put them away.

_____

4. Peggy took the hot roast out to serve her guests.

_____

5. Don opened a can of soup, then added water, and warmed it up.

_____

2 Dictionary Work

●
●○ Choose words that fit the following definitions.

1. an appliance used to mix, combine, or chop various foods and liquids   _____

2. a tool used to roll out dough on a flat surface   _____

3. a small box or can for holding a dry product   _____

4. a bowl-like utensil with holes for draining food   _____

5. a dish in which food can be baked and served   _____

6. a small piece of rough material used to clean dirty pots and pans   _____

3 More Dictionary Work

A word may have several meanings. Here are two words given as dictionary entries. Look at all the definitions and circle the one that refers to the kitchen.

1. counter
   a) a piece of material used for counting in games
   b) a person who counts
   c) a flat surface on which food is prepared

2. cabinet
   a) a cupboard with doors and shelves
   b) a group of advisors for the head of a government
   c) a small room in a museum

4 Kitchen Sayings

Can you figure out what these sayings mean? Explain them on another sheet of paper. Then add a kitchen saying from your part of the world and explain it.

1. The pot calls the kettle black.

2. Out of the frying pan and into the fire.

21

Kitchen Verbs page 31

1 Fill in the Blanks

Find the best words to fit into the blanks. Review page **30** before you begin.

1. Kathy will _____ some water into a saucepan.

2. Mother can _____ three loaves of bread in the oven at the same time.

3. They decided to use a cutting board to _____ and _____ the vegetables.

4. We will _____ the chicken in the large iron frying pan.

5. She wants to _____ the eggs into a mixing bowl and then

   _____ them until they are white and fluffy.

6. She told us to _____ food often so it wouldn't stick.

2 Preparation

How do you fix your favorite foods? Fill in the chart. You may use words from pages **6–12.**

	BOIL	BAKE	CHOP	PEEL	SLICE
1. _____					
2. _____					
3. _____					
4. _____					
5. _____					

3   Mystery Conversations

From what they are saying, decide what these people are doing or are about to do. There may be more than one good answer.

> Lisa: How many potatoes will you need for the soup?
>
> Frank: About ten, I think.
>
> Lisa: OK, I'll fix them.

1. *Lisa is peeling potatoes.*

> Joe: I think the steaks are burning!
>
> Pat: Oh, my goodness, you're right! Open the oven door quickly!

2. _____

> Mother: How much milk do you want, Bobby?
>
> Bobby: Just half a glass, Mom.

3. _____

> Jerry: The onions are making me cry!
>
> Kathy: Put some lemon juice on your knife — it will help!

4. _____

> Mother: Give Grandpa the biggest piece, dear.
>
> Father: OK, this is the biggest piece of turkey I have cut.

5. _____

4   A Recipe

Write down a recipe for food that you know how to make. It might be as easy as toast or as hard as cheesecake! Tell exactly what to do. Use as many kitchen verbs as possible.

22 The Bedroom page 32

1 Change the Sheets

How do you make a bed? Put the sentences in the correct order.

_____ Then put the flat sheet on the bed.
_____ Then put the fitted sheet on the bed.
_____ Put the bedspread on top of the blanket.
___1___ Take off the dirty sheets.
_____ Place the pillows in the pillowcases.
_____ Put the comforter at the foot of the bed.
_____ Put the blanket on the bed.
_____ Put the pillows on the bed.

2 A New Look

Read the following paragraph and underline all the words from page 32.

Randy and Norma Chiu decided to redecorate their bedroom. The curtains and bedspread used to be yellow; now they are blue. They decided to take down the blinds and put up new draw curtains. They chose light green sheets and pillowcases to go with the blue bedspread. They replaced the double bed with a king-sized bed and threw away the headboard and footboard. Their bureau and chest of drawers used to be in dark wood, but yesterday they bought new ones, painted black. Last winter, Norma made a lovely dark green comforter, but they put it away because the weather was too warm for it then. They'll probably take it out in a week or so. Finally, Randy wants to call the telephone company tomorrow to order a blue phone for the bedroom. The jack is already there, so there's nothing to do but plug in the cord. They're sure they'll enjoy the new look of their bedroom.

3 Questions

Answer these questions on another sheet of paper.

1. What do they have to cover their bedroom window?

2. What kind of furniture do they have now?

3. What used to be yellow?

4. What did they put away for a while?

5. What will Randy order tomorrow?

1 Help!

List any items from page 33 that might be useful in these situations.

1. Change the baby's diapers! _____

2. The baby is hungry! _____

3. The baby is unhappy and crying! _____

4. The baby is sleepy! _____

5. Take the baby for a walk! _____

2 Dear Doctor Brock

The following problems were taken from letters written to a famous baby doctor. Help the doctor give good advice by filling in the blanks with words from page 33. There may be several good answers.

1. Whenever the phone rings, I'm afraid to leave the baby to answer it. If I take the baby with me, he screams so loudly that I can't hear!

   Put the baby in a _____ and give it a _____ to play with.

2. Our baby is just starting to walk, and she falls a lot. We're afraid she'll hurt herself. What should we do?

   Buy a _____ for her to walk in so she can't hurt herself.

3. Our daughter just had a baby. Our son-in-law smokes, and we're afraid our daughter's house is not safe from fire. What do you suggest?

   All houses should have a _____ _____ whether there's a baby in the house or not.

4. Yesterday I overheard my sister tell my mother that my baby didn't smell as good as her baby. I was angry, but maybe she's right! What's your advice?

   Many parents use _____ _____ and _____

   _____ to help keep their babies smelling sweet.

3 The Baby Shower

Replace the ten italicized sections with words from page 33.
Write them on the lines below.

Fifteen women went to a baby shower to give Sara presents for her new baby. Sara hoped they would give her a (1) *table to change the baby's diapers on* and (2) *something colorful to hang above the baby's crib.* She didn't get those, but she did get lots of other gifts. She got a (3) *chair with wheels for pushing,* a (4) *box to put the baby's toys in,* and many cute (5) *outfits for the baby to sleep in.* Her sister gave her a (6) *large bed for the baby* as well as a (7) *smaller baby bed.* Many friends gave her toys: a (8) *toy that makes noise,* (9) *toys that have the ABCs on them,* and (10) *toys that are soft and nice to hold.* It was a great party for Sara.

1. _____

2. _____

3. _____

4. _____

5. _____

6. _____

7. _____

8. _____

9. _____

10. _____

4 Stop Crying!

On another sheet of paper, describe three ways you would try to stop a baby from crying. Be specific, and use as many words from page 33 as possible. Use the words *first*, *second*, and *third*.

44

24 The Bathroom page 34

1 Bathroom Courtesy

●
○○ Choose a word from page 34 to complete these good bathroom rules. There may be more than one answer.

1. Don't leave hair in the _____ .

2. Put the cap on the _____ when you're finished with it.

3. Hang up the _____ _____ when you're finished with your bath.

4. Put the soap back in the _____ _____ when you're done washing.

5. Put all your dirty clothes in the _____ .

6. Put out a new roll of _____ _____ when you finish a roll.

7. Clean out the _____ after you take a bath.

8. Don't splatter toothpaste all over the _____ .

2 Odd Man Out

●
●○ Circle the word that doesn't belong and tell why.

1. hamper   bathtub   (tile)   wastepaper basket   *It isn't a container.*

2. shampoo   stopper   soap   toothpaste _____

3. sponge   washcloth   mirror   towel _____

4. nailbrush   toilet brush   toothbrush _____

5. scale   faucet   bathtub   shower head _____

3 Endless Stories

●
●● Read the following situations. Tell what the person did next.
Finish the story in two or three sentences. Use all of the given words.

1. Sam was taking a shower. Suddenly, the phone rang.

    shower curtain, bathtub, bath towel

*He pulled back the shower curtain and climbed out of the bathtub. Then
he grabbed a bath towel and ran to answer the phone.*

45

2. Lisa was taking a shower. Suddenly, the hot water stopped!

   cold water faucet, hot water faucet, bathtub, bath towel

_____

_____

3. Betty answered the phone at 7 p.m. It was Frank. He asked if she'd like to go to a movie with him at 8 p.m. Betty said yes, but after she hung up, she remembered that her hair was dirty and messy.

   sink, hand towel, shampoo, hair dryer

_____

_____

4. Joe's mother just called him. She told him that she was on her way over to see his new apartment. She said she'd be there in an hour. Joe's apartment is a mess, especially the bathroom!

   hamper, bathtub, sink, mirror, toilet, toilet brush, wastepaper basket

_____

_____

_____

_____

4 On Your Own

Write a paragraph about what you do when you get up in the morning. Use the words below, and words like *first, second, third, then, after that,* and *finally*. Then write four questions about your paragraph. Give your paragraph and questions to a partner to see if he/she can answer your questions correctly.

hair dryer	toothbrush	sponge	bath towel	toothpaste
mirror	hair brush	comb	jewelry box	night table
closet	hanger	hook	soap	shampoo
alarm clock	box of tissues	floor	light switch	blanket
washcloth	bathtub	shower		

25 The Utility Room page 35

1 Safety First

Pick a partner. Look at the items on page 35 and decide which ones might be dangerous. Give reasons for why you think they might cause problems. Together, give a short report to the rest of the class on what you decided.

2 Good Beginnings

For each beginning, choose the best ending.

__d__ 1. They like soft clothes,   a. so they got out a plunger.

____ 2. They like very white clothes,   b. so they got out the mop and bucket.

____ 3. The light went out,   c. so they always add bleach to the wash.

____ 4. They spilled a pot of coffee,   d. so they always add fabric softener.

____ 5. The toilet was stopped up,   e. so they put in a new lightbulb.

____ 6. They like their collars to stand up, f. so they used starch.

3 The Perfect Ending

Complete these sentences. Use the sentences in exercise 1 as examples. Use as many words from page 35 as possible. There may be more than one good ending.

1. Her clothes were all wrinkled, *so she got out the ironing board and iron.*

2. The electricity went out, _____

3. He saw a mouse in the house last week, _____

4. She couldn't reach the ceiling lightbulb, _____

5. She dropped some dirt on the carpet, _____

6. The dryer didn't work, _____

7. The kitchen sink was dirty, _____

8. The mop sponge is old and dirty, _____

9. I didn't have any rags to clean with, _____

4 From Start to Finish

Now write entire sentences like the ones in exercise 3. Use the two words given below.

1. drain/plunger

_____

2. circuit breaker/flashlight

_____

3. garbage/garbage can

_____

4. window/window cleaner

_____

5. vacuum cleaner/broom

_____

6. dust/dustpan

_____

5 Cleanup Time!

Think of the way your house or apartment looks right now. Pretend that your English teacher is going to visit you this evening, and you want the place to look its best. Write a paragraph on the three cleaning jobs you would do today after you got home from school and explain those jobs.

1 A Hard Job

You have a job to do. Which tools would you choose? You may
choose several, and you may use a word more than once.

1. Fix a leaky pipe.   *wrench, pliers,* _____

2. Make a wooden table. _____

3. Replace a wall switch. _____

4. Hang a heavy picture on a wall. _____

5. Pull out some nails from a wall. _____

6. Refinish an old chair. _____

7. Fix a broken window. _____

2 The Room That Jack Painted

Read the following paragraph. Find five tools that are not used
correctly and cross them out. Write the name of the correct tool
on the lines to the right.

Jack decided to paint his living room. The old paint was peeling
off, so he used a drill to remove it. Then he used a mallet to make
the walls smooth. He used a small piece of sandpaper to do the
corners. He decided to use a saw instead of a paintbrush, and since
he already had the pan, all he had to buy was paint. Before he
began, he decided to remove all the switch plates from the walls
with a hammer. He looked around his workshop and finally found
one lying on his workbench. Soon he was ready to paint. That job
was easy. When he finished, he put back all the switch plates. That
job was hard because he could not find the old screws, and he
didn't have the right-sized wrench.

1. _____

2. _____

3. _____

4. _____

5. _____

3 The Dictionary Workshop

Here are some expressions that use workshop vocabulary. See
if you can find out what they mean in a larger dictionary. Write
their meanings on another sheet of paper.

1. He's nuts!
2. Can you nail down the cost?
3. That'll throw a monkey wrench into it.
4. Learn the nuts and bolts of English!
5. The police nailed the robber.
6. She hit the nail on the head.
7. She's a live wire.
8. He painted the town red.

1 Household Chores

Answer these questions. Follow the examples.

A. What can you do to these items?

1. floor   *Sweep it.*

2. mirror _____

3. bed _____

4. wet dishes _____

5. bathtub _____

6. laundry _____

B. What can you do with these items?

1. soap   *Wash with it.*

2. paper towels _____

3. cleanser _____

4. hammer _____

5. clothespin _____

6. wrench _____

2 Question and Answer Time

Answer the following questions.

1. Name something you can wash and iron. _____

2. What do you need in order to vacuum? _____

3. Name four things you can dust. _____

4. Name three things you can change. _____

5. Name three things you can dry with. _____

6. Name four things you can wipe with. _____

3 A Busy Schedule

The Simpson family has a lot planned for the month of May. Look at the calendar on the opposite page. Add four reminders for them about the jobs they have to do in order to be ready for visits, meetings, etc. One note has already been included for May 27th.

M A Y						
SUNDAY	MONDAY	TUESDAY	WEDNESDAY	THURSDAY	FRIDAY	SATURDAY
					1	2
3	4	5	6 7:30 Business meeting at house	7	8	9
10 Grandma visits	11	12	13	14	15 Mary's Birthday Party 8:00	16
17	18 ← Out	of town	guests →	21	22	23
24 31	25	26	27 WASH CLOTHES	28 Trip to	the mountains (500 mi) 29	30

4 Preparation Paragraph

On another sheet of paper, write a paragraph on all the chores the Simpson family has to do in May. You might want to start out with a sentence like this—*There are a lot of household chores for the Simpson family to do if they want to be prepared in the month of May.*

1 First Things First

●
○○ Look at the pairs of sentences. Decide which action came first. Circle that sentence.

1. The doctor put a cast on her leg.   They took an X ray.

2. He sat on the examining table.   The doctor listened with a stethoscope.

3. The nurse filled the syringe.   The doctor stuck the needle in his arm.

4. The oral hygienist put the instruments on a tray.   The dentist took a mirror and looked into her mouth.

5. The doctor began to take stitches.   The nurse cleaned his arm with alcohol.

2 Order, Please!

●
●○ Read the following sentences. Number them according to time order. The first one is done.

A.

_____ So the attendants helped her to a wheelchair.

__1__ The patient tried to use the crutches, but she couldn't.

_____ The nurse began to look at her chart.

_____ They wheeled her into the examining room.

B.

_____ She washed his cut with alcohol.

_____ The nurse took off the Band-Aid.

_____ The patient had a Band-Aid on his arm.

_____ She put a clean gauze bandage on his arm.

C.

_____ The dentist pushed the pedal and the chair moved back.

_____ The patient used the basin.

_____ The dentist used the drill.

_____ The patient sat in the dentist's chair.

3 A Talk With the Doctor

Finish the conversations by filling in the blanks.

1. A: "Doctor, what will you do to my arm?"

   B: "I'll take an _____ _____ of it, and if it's broken, I'll put

      on a _____ ___ and put your arm in a _____."

2. A: "Doctor, what's that thing hanging around your neck?" asked
      the little boy.

   B: "It's called a _____, and with it I can hear your
      heart beating."

4 A Frightening Experience?

The doctor's or dentist's office can be a frightening place.
Choose two or three items from page 39 that most people are
afraid of or dislike a lot. Write a short paragraph on why they
dislike them, and whether you also are afraid of them. Start
your paragraph with: *Many people hate to go to the doctor's or
dentist's office*.

1 You're the Doctor

Match the following complaints and remedies.

_____ 1. I have a cold.
_____ 2. I think I broke my arm.
_____ 3. I've sprained my ankle!
_____ 4. Look at this black eye!
_____ 5. I have a terrible backache.

a. Here's a heating pad.
b. You need an ice pack.
c. Get plenty of bedrest.
d. Let's take an X ray.
e. Let's put a stretch bandage on.

2 Medical Record Form

Fill out this form as if you were doing it for your doctor's records.

1. Do you often have headaches? _____ If so, how often? _____

2. Have you ever had a fever? _____ If so, how often? _____

3. Have you ever broken a bone? _____ If so, which one(s)? _____

4. Have you ever had surgery? _____ If so, what kind? _____

5. Do you often have sore throats? _____ If so, for how long? _____

6. Do you take any medication (pills/tablets/capsules)?_____

   If so, what kind? _____

7. Do you take any medication by injection? _____ If so, what kind? _____

8. Do you know your blood pressure? _____ If so, what is it? _____

9. Do you bruise easily? _____

10. Do you get rashes from any foods? _____ If so, which food(s)? _____

3 Idioms

Choose a partner and, with the help of a larger dictionary, find out what the following sentences mean. Write their meanings on another sheet of paper.

1. That news is a bitter pill to swallow.
2. That horror movie gave me the chills.
3. When my boss said I was doing well, it was a real shot in the arm.
4. My old friend was a sight for sore eyes.
5. There has been a rash of new workers in the factory.

1 Hot Lines

Read these conversations. What item are the people talking about? There may be more than one good answer.

1. A: I smell smoke.
   B: I do, too!

   They are talking about fire.

2. A: His head wasn't injured.
   B: It's good that he was wearing one!

   _____

3. A: She has a very hard job.
   B: Yes, but think of all the people she has saved.

   _____

4. A: We need one to break the windows!
   B: There's one in the back of the fire truck.

   _____

5. A: Every tall building should have one.
   B: Yes, it's another way to leave a tall building.

   _____

6. A: Get the water closer to the fire!
   B: It's not long enough!

   _____

2 Where There's Smoke There's Fire!

Fill in the blanks in this story with words from page 42. You may use words more than once. End it by writing some of your own sentences on another sheet of paper.

Last January, there was a fire on the second floor of my apartment building. A

_____ _____ arrived only six minutes after the _____

started. The _____ _____ found a woman trying to put out the fire

with a _____ _____. It was not enough. They returned to the street

and connected a _____ to the _____ _____ outside our

building. Soon ___ _____ filled the building, and it was hard to breathe. The fire fighters

put a _____ up to the second floor, carried up a heavy _____, and then

broke the window with an _____. They pumped lots of water on the fire. Many

people left the building by way of the _____ _____. A few people

were injured, so they had to call an _____.

1 Your Choice

Read these sentence beginnings. Circle the best ending for each beginning.

1. The police officer showed
   a. her badge to the judge.
   b. his jury box to the defendant.

2. The detective found
   a. no fingerprints on the gun.
   b. no robes in the jail.

3. The judge said the
   a. witness must go to jail.
   b. defendant must go to jail.

4. The judge hit
   a. the jury box with his robes.
   b. the table with his gavel.

5. The police officer had to hit
   a. the suspect with his nightstick.
   b. the transcript with her badge.

6. The detective put his
   a. handcuffs into his holster.
   b. gun into his holster.

2 Who Said It?

Read the following quotes. Decide who is talking.

1. Ten years in jail!   *the judge*

2. All 12 of us believe the defendant is guilty. _____

3. I saw the suspect rob the bank. _____

4. I will prove that the defendant did it. _____

5. I caught her and put the handcuffs on her. _____

6. I will prove that the defendant didn't do it. _____

3 The Perfect Ending

Add your own endings to each of these sentence beginnings. Use the words given in parentheses.

1. (witness stand) The prosecuting attorney *walked to the witness stand*.

2. (jail) The suspect _____

3. (court) The judge _____

4. (witness stand) The witness _____

56

32 The City pages 44–45

1 Giving Directions

Look at the picture in the Dictionary. You know this city very well. As people ask you questions about places in the city, direct them. Use the prepositions *across from* or *next to*.

1. Where's the bakery?   *It's next to the department store.*

2. Where's the parking garage?   _____

3. Where's the newsstand?   _____

4. Where's the fruit market?   _____

5. Where's a trash basket?   _____

6. Where's the bus stop?   _____

2 General City Questions

Answer these questions about the picture with complete sentences. There may be more than one good answer.

1. What do people walk on in the city?   7. What is at 201 Main Street?

People walk on sidewalks.   _____

2. Where can I throw out some paper?   8. Where can I buy a birthday cake?

_____   _____

3. Where can I catch a subway?   9. What is at most busy intersections?

_____   _____

4. Where do I look for street names?   10. Where do people live in the city?

_____   _____

5. Where can I buy medicine?   11. Where do many people work?

_____   _____

6. What do babies often ride in?   12. Where can I buy a magazine?

_____   _____

13. What changes from red to green?

_____

14. Where can I find a good book?

_____

15. Where should you cross the street?

_____

16. Where's a good place to sit?

_____

17. Who directs traffic?

_____

3 You Are There!

Read the following conversations and decide where the people
are. Use the prepositions *in*, *on*, or *by*.

1. A: How much money should I put in?   B: A dime is enough. We won't be gone long.
   They're by a parking meter.

2. A: Watch out, there's a car coming!   B: He didn't see us crossing!

_____

3. A: How much do the cookies cost?   B: They're $1.50 a dozen.

_____

4. A: Fourth floor, please.   B: I want that floor, too!

_____

5. A: Let me call Dan and tell him I'll be late.   B: OK, you can call from here.

_____

6. A: Don't throw that away on the street!   B: Throw it in here!

_____

7. A: Look both ways before you cross.   B: OK, Mommy.

_____

8. A: When do you think the number 5 will come?   B: It will be here in five minutes.

_____

4 Lots to Do

Look at these things that Kim must do and buy. Then look at the picture. Write a paragraph explaining how Kim will get everything done. Tell where she will walk and what she will pass. She will start at the parking garage. Use words like *first, second, third, then, next, after that,* and *finally.* Try to use 15 words from pages 44–45.

Buy	Do
newspaper, blouse, cosmetics,	call her boyfriend
oranges, and pears	mail a letter

5 My City

No cities or towns are perfect. Think of the city or town where you are from. Explain three or four things that you like about it and three or four things that you don't like about it.

Things I Like	Things I Don't Like
_____	_____
_____	_____
_____	_____

1 Help!

You must do the following jobs. Decide what you'll need.

Need

1. Send a package to a friend. · *label, tape, string*

2. You're on vacation. Send a card. _____

3. Send a letter to another country. _____

4. Send a friend some money by mail. _____

5. Your sister's birthday is tomorrow, and you forgot to send her the gift you bought. _____

2 Rules to Remember

Use the following words to write five rules about mailing letters, postcards, and packages. You may use a word more than once. Try to use all the words somewhere in the five sentences.

mail	stamp	return address	packages	string
letter	tape	mailbox	zip code	envelope

1. *Remember to put your mail into the mailbox on time.*

2. _____

3. _____

4. _____

5. _____

3 The Letter Carrier

Fill in the blanks in the following story. Use any of the words on page 46. Do not use a word more than once.

The _____ _____ took her _____ from the

_____ _____ and began to walk down the street. When she got to the

Martin house, she took a box out of her bag and rang the bell. "Here's a _____ for

you," she said to Mrs. Martin. Mrs. Martin thanked her, and the letter carrier left. Later, Mrs.

Martin saw that the box was not for her. "Wait a minute," she said to herself. "This is the right

_____ and _____ _____ on the _____, but

this is not my name." It was addressed to Mrs. Martinez. She used to be Mrs. Martin's neighbor

until she moved away. Mrs. Martin looked at the _____ _____ to see if

she knew the person who sent it. She didn't know that person. The _____ showed

that it had been mailed the day before.

   Mrs. Martin ran after the letter carrier, but she had already left. So Mrs. Martin took the box to

the _____ _____. She stood in line for about five minutes and then

went up to the _____. She told the _____ _____ what

had happened. He took the box and marked it RETURN TO SENDER.

4 You Decide!

Answer these questions about the story in exercise 3 on
another sheet of paper. The story may not give you the exact
answer, so you may have to guess. Use at least one word from
page 46 in each answer.

1. Why didn't the letter carrier put the box in Mrs. Martin's
   mailbox?

2. Why didn't Mrs. Martin give the box right back to the letter
   carrier?

3. How did Mrs. Martin know the box was not for her?

4. Why didn't Mrs. Martin mark RETURN TO SENDER on the box,
   put it by her front door, and let the letter carrier pick it up the
   next day?

1 Odd Man Out

Circle the word that does not belong. Tell why.

1. encyclopedia   dictionary   (magazine)   *It's not a reference book.*

2. photocopy machine   microfilm reader   subject _____

3. title   call number   author   globe _____

4. library card   periodicals section   reference section _____

2 Information, Please!

You work at the information desk of your local library. Help out the people who ask the following questions by writing directions on another sheet of paper. There may be more than one good answer.

1. Where can I find the magazine *Reader's Choice*?

   Look in the periodicals section.

2. Where do I go to take out this book?

3. I need to see a map of Asia.

4. What's the meaning of "anthology"?

5. Where can I find the call cards?

6. I need to find a book by Mark Twain.

7. Where can I find information on the history of the United States?

8. Where is Japan in relation to England?

9. Where will I find the encyclopedias, atlases, dictionaries, and maps?

10. Can someone help me find some reference books?

11. I have the call number for the book I want. Where will I find the book?

12. Which part of the card catalog will help me find books on medical care?

3 Research

You are going to write a paper on George Washington for your English teacher. You don't know anything about him, so you decide to visit the public library. Explain how you would find information about George Washington. Write several paragraphs with lots of details. Use words like *first, second, after that, then, next, before that,* and *finally.*

35 The Armed Forces page 48

1 Definitions

● Find a word from page 48 for each definition below.
○○

1. a member of the Army _____

2. a knife-like attachment to a rifle _____

3. an underwater ship _____

4. what you pull to fire a rifle _____

5. the part of the gun where the bullet travels _____

6. a submarine instrument to see above water _____

7. the branch of the armed forces to which sailors belong _____

8. an explosive dropped from the air _____

9. an explosive thrown by hand _____

10. an Army vehicle for transport _____

2 Follow the Order!

●● Put these groups of four sentences into chronological order.
●○

A.
_____ The airman jumped out of the plane with his parachute.
_____ Friendly soldiers found him on the ground.
_____ The fighter plane was hit.
_____ The enemy shot bullets at the airman from the ground.

B.
_____ He saw an aircraft carrier in the distance.
_____ The submarine went through the water just below the surface.
_____ He plotted a new course to avoid it.
_____ The captain raised the periscope to see if there were any ships nearby.

3 Groupings

●
●● Choose a word or words from each section on page 48 and
form sentences like this example: *A sailor shot a shell from a battleship.*

1 What's My Line?

Find a partner and decide what kind of truck you would like to drive. Write it down on another sheet of paper. Join another pair of students, and see if you can guess what kind of truck they have chosen by asking three yes/no questions. Then have them try to guess yours!

2 The Truckers' Cafe

The following comments were overheard at the local truckers' cafe. Read each comment, decide what kind of driver is talking, and write what kind of truck he/she drives.

1. Trash cans are very heavy!

   A sanitation worker who drives a garbage truck.

2. Delivering oil is a dangerous job!

   _____

3. I've moved five rooms of furniture today!

   _____

4. I'm on my way to pull a broken-down car to a service station.

   _____

5. They bought a lot of hamburgers today!

   _____

6. I still have six more packages to deliver.

   _____

7. I have seven new automobiles on the truck.

   _____

8. I hope it doesn't snow again tomorrow!

   _____

9. I'm loaded with two tons of dirt!

_____

10. The mixer makes so much noise!

_____

11. You wouldn't believe how dirty the city streets are!

_____

3 Dear Gabby

The person who wrote the following letter has a problem. Read
the letter and pretend you are Gabby. Write a good answer,
giving your best advice on what to do and what not to do. Use
as many words from page 49 as possible in your answer.

Dear Gabby,

I've been a mover for 15
years. I hurt my back lifting
a heavy refrigerator and have
not been able to work since. My
doctor says I can't do any more
heavy lifting. All I have ever done
is move furniture. Since I like
to drive trucks and am good at
it, I would like to find
another job driving. What kind of
work do you think I ought to
try? I must find a job because
my family needs the money!

Sincerely

37 Cars pages 50–51

1 What Do You Call It?

Look at the picture of the car interior in the Dictionary. Read the sentence beginnings and decide which item you would use or look at. Complete each sentence. There may be more than one good answer.

1. When you want to rest your neck,   use the *headrest*.

2. When you park on a hill,   _____

3. When the sun is in your eyes,   _____

4. When you want to see how fast you're going,   look at the _____

5. When you want to see the driver behind you,   _____

6. When you want fresh air,   _____

7. When you want to start the car,   _____

8. When you want to be safe in an accident,   _____

9. When you want to see if you're out of gas,   _____

10. When a dog runs out in front of you,   _____

11. When you want to see how far you've gone,   _____

12. When you want to make a turn,   _____

13. When you want to speed up,   _____

14. When you want to shift gears,   _____

15. When you want to put a map away,   _____

2 You Be the Mechanic

Here are some problems that friends tell you they're having with their cars. What do you think is wrong? There may be more than one good answer. You may use an answer more than once.

1. There's a loud knock in the engine.   *It may be the fan belt.*

2. The stations on my radio don't come in clearly. _____

3. The temperature indicator light is on. _____

4. I smell gasoline. _____

5. My car is leaking cooling water. _____

6. My tires squeal when I make a turn. _____

7. The dipstick came out almost dry. _____

8. All of my lights are dim. _____

3 Insurance Claims

Insurance companies must know what kind of damage
accidents cause. You work for an insurance company. Decide
which parts of the cars were probably damaged.

Situation	What was damaged?

1. Mary ran over some glass in the
   street. She had a blowout, lost control
   of the car, and hit a tree. After changing
   her tire, she was able to drive the car
   home without trouble.

   _____
   _____
   _____
   _____
   _____

2. Tom was traveling 25 mph and was
   hit head-on by an oncoming car. He
   could not drive the car home. There was
   glass and water all over the street.

   _____
   _____
   _____
   _____

3. Sherry was leaving a parking space
   at the supermarket and backed into
   another car. She left her name on the
   other car's windshield and drove home.

   _____
   _____
   _____
   _____

4. Bart was driving along a city street and
   didn't see a red light. He had to stop
   suddenly. The car in back of him hit
   him hard. Bart was able to drive home.

   _____
   _____
   _____
   _____

4 Buying a Car

 Read the following paragraph and answer the questions.

When you shop for a car, you must check to see that it drives well. But, in addition to this, you should make sure that the car is safe and comfortable on the inside. For example, find out if the instruments on the dashboard are easy to read and well lit at night. Make sure the glove compartment is large enough for your needs. Check to see that you can adjust the driver's seat so that the steering wheel is not too high or too low. Be sure to sit in the seats long enough to know that they are comfortable, and make sure the seat belts are easy to fasten and unfasten. It is a good idea to check the door locks on all the doors, and if you often drive children, it might be good to get a car with "child-proof" door locks on the back doors. Take the car on a test drive and see that the turn signal lights, emergency brake, and indicator lights work. Check to see that there are enough vents if you live in a hot area and need air conditioning. It's better to spend a little time checking your car before you buy it than to be sorry afterward.

1. Name two things to check that have to do with comfort.

_____

2. Name three things to check that have to do with safety.

_____

3. What do you suppose "child-proof" door locks mean?

_____

4. Why might it be bad if the steering wheel is too high? Too low?

_____

5. Who needs to check the vents carefully?

_____

38 Bikes page 52

1 Buying a Bike

Read the following descriptions of bikes and people looking for bikes. Then choose the best bike for each person.

A. motor scooter

B. tricycle

C. three-speed woman's bicycle

D. dirt bike

E. full-sized motorcycle

F. child's bike with training wheels

1. _____ Timmy is three years old, and his parents are looking for his first bike.

2. _____ Susan is seventeen, and she is looking for a quick way to go back and forth to high school and her part-time job. Her bicycle is too slow, and her parents are afraid of fast motorcycles.

3. _____ Lisa wants to get more exercise. A friend recommended that she ride a bike several times a week. She's looking for a good buy—she doesn't have much money.

4. _____ Dave just got a new job in a city fifteen miles away. He doesn't have enough money for a car. He needs a cheap, fast way to get to work.

5. _____ Jerry is fourteen years old, and his parents are looking for a strong bike that he can use on hilly dirt roads.

6. _____ Sandy is six years old and has never had a bike before. Her parents are looking for a safe bike for Sandy to ride.

2 Bicycle Care and Safety

Read the following paragraphs and answer the questions.

Here are some things that everyone should know about bike care and safety. First of all, bicycles should be kept in good condition and well-equipped. For example, be sure that the brakes work well. If you have hand brakes, check them often. Also, be sure to check for flat tires or tires that are losing air. Always carry a hand pump with you. Otherwise, you might have to walk a long distance! You may ruin your wheels if you ride with a flat tire. All bikes should have horns for emergency situations, and, of course, all bikes should have reflectors for nighttime riding. You can never be sure when you will have to ride your bike, so it's best to be prepared. Be sure that your chain is covered, and, to be safe, always tie the bottom of your pants leg if you're wearing pants.

When you ride your bike, never carry passengers on the handlebars or fenders because this is dangerous. Always pedal your bike with the traffic and never against it. Wear a helmet and carry a good lock and cable. Always lock your bike in a bike stand if there is one nearby. Do these things and you will enjoy using your bicycle.

1. Name three things to carry with you.

2. Why are reflectors a good idea?

3. Name two things to check for.

4. Why should chains be covered?

5. Why are passengers on the handlebars or fenders dangerous?

6. Why is it a good idea to wear a helmet?

3 The Perfect Bike

Think of your own situation and needs. Describe the bike that would be most useful for you.

1 Word Scramble

Look at the picture in the Dictionary. Then unscramble the following sentences on another sheet of paper.

1. a is A behind camper trailer

2. exit truck will A soon

3. near hitchhiker is speed limit A sign the

4. is a overpass car on There the

5. ahead A is of motorcycle a van

6. bus behind a is passenger A car

7. area are in two cars the service There

8. tollbooth the driver is A at paying

2 Driver's License Test

Choose the best answer for each question.

1. Never drive on the _____.
   a. shoulder of the road
   b. the right lane
   c. the left lane

2. Slow down as you get to the _____.
   a. cloverleaf
   b. center divider
   c. exit ramp

3. Never cross _____.
   a. an overpass
   b. a cloverleaf
   c. the center divider

4. When you hear an emergency vehicle, pull into the _____.
   a. left lane
   b. right lane
   c. tollbooth

5. Get onto an interstate highway from _____.
   a. an entrance ramp
   b. an exit ramp
   c. a service area

6. Slower traffic should stay in the _____.
   a. left lane
   b. center lane
   c. right lane

7. Always obey the _____.
   a. gas pump
   b. speed limit
   c. exit sign

8. If your car breaks down, pull onto the road's _____.
   a. shoulder
   b. entrance ramp
   c. air pump

9. Always stop at _____.
   a. service areas
   b. exit signs
   c. tollbooths

10. Vehicles in the right lane must watch out for cars on the _____.
    a. exit ramps
    b. entrance ramps
    c. overpasses

3 Traffic Problems

Look at the picture again. On another sheet of paper, give the drivers in the following situations exact directions to accomplish what they want to do.

1. The motorcycle wants to exit at the cloverleaf.

2. The van wants to use the service area.

3. The car on the overpass wants to get on the interstate highway.

4. The car at the gas pumps needs air in its tires.

4 Emergency

Have you ever had a bad experience on a highway? Write a paragraph about your worst experience on the road.

1 Category Search

Find words for each of the following categories. Write your answers on the lines below.

1. Seven people

_____

2. Four things made of paper

_____

3. Two things that cost money

_____

4. Nine forms of public transportation

_____

5. Two things to pull or hold

_____

6. Five forms of public transportation that run on a track

_____

2 Cultural Questions

Choose the best answer and tell why you chose it. There may be more than one good answer.

1. An elderly man gets on a crowded bus. A middle-aged woman rider should
   a. get up and motion to her seat.
   b. stay seated and say nothing.
   c. ask if he would like her seat.
   d. other

2. A taxicab driver gives you your change in ten-dollar bills. You don't have any smaller change, and you don't want to tip ten dollars.
   a. Ask the driver if he has change.
   b. Leave no tip.
   c. Ask the driver to wait a minute and get change from a nearby store.
   d. Other

3. The driver of a horse-drawn carriage has given you a very nice
   tour of the city. Give
   a. a 5% tip.
   b. a 15% tip.
   c. no tip.
   d. other

4. The person next to you on the train is sitting very close to you,
   and you begin to feel uncomfortable.
   a. Pull the emergency cord.
   b. Change your seat.
   c. Leave the train.
   d. Tell the conductor.
   e. Other

3 Plus or Minus

Decide if each of the sentences below is an advantage or a
disadvantage for that type of public transportation. Put a plus
in front of the advantages and a minus in front of the
disadvantages.

Bus   _____ Riders must always have correct change for the fare box.
           _____ Riders can get transfers from one bus route to another.

Subway   _____ The conductors speak fast, and it's hard to understand them.
           _____ During rush hours there are many subways to choose from.

Train   _____ Commuter trains never have to go through traffic.
           _____ Train timetables are long and difficult to understand.

Taxi   _____ Taxi fares are expensive, and the passenger must tip the driver.
           _____ Taxicabs are often the quickest way to get around in the city.

4 The Question, Please!

Write a good question for each of the following answers on the
lines below. Follow the example.

1. Ask the bus driver.   *What do you do if you're not sure of your stop?*

2. Pull the cord! _____

3. Hold onto the strap. _____

4. Look at the timetable. _____

5. Look at the meter. _____

6. Take a horse-drawn carriage. _____

7. Ask the conductor. _____

8. Give a good tip. _____

9. Go to a taxi stand. _____

10. Listen to the conductor. _____

11. Offer your seat. _____

5 Transportation Survey

Find out the answers to the following questions. Write your
findings and report them to the class.

1. Where is the closest bus stop to your school? ____ _____

_____

2. What is the bus fare in your town/city? ____ _____

How much is a transfer? _____

3. Is there a subway in the nearest large city? _____ If not, why not?

_____

4. Does a commuter train run through your town/city? _____ If so, get a
timetable and find out when it stops in your town.

5. What is the name of the taxi company that serves your town/city?

_____

What is the base fare? _____ What is the fare per mile? _____

How much would it cost to go by taxi to the closest airport? _____

6. Are there any "other" forms of public transportation
(see section E on page 55) in your town/city?

_____

41 Air Travel page 56

1 Quotes Match

Match the following quotes to the people who might say them.
Choose from the people on page 56.

_____ 1. Put your carry-on bag on the conveyor belt.

_____ 2. May I see your boarding pass?

_____ 3. This is Captain Miller speaking from the cockpit.

_____ 4. Oh, no, I think I've lost my ticket!

_____ 5. I'll put your baggage on the dolly.

_____ 6. Please put up your tray table, we're about to land.

_____ 7. Would you go through the metal detector again, please?

_____ 8. Where can I put my garment bag?

2 Dialogue Completion

Connie and Pete Wallace are about to take their first plane trip.
Fill in the blanks in the following conversation with their
travel agent.

Pete: What's the easiest way to check in?

Agent: Go directly to the _____ _____. Someone will tear off a

            part of your _____ and give you your

            _____ _____ so that you can get on the plane. He'll also

            take all of the _____ that you want to check.

Connie: How many _____ _____ can we take on the plane

            with us?

Agent: You can take two, but remember, anything you take on the plane will have to go

            through the _____ _____.

76

Pete: Oh, that's right. Will that hurt my film?

Agent: It shouldn't, but it's best to ask the _____ _____. Also, it's

good to remember that all carry-on bags must fit under your seat or into the

_____ _____.

3 A Smooth Trip

Write a paragraph about the woman in the picture. Answer the following questions in your paragraph. Be sure to name the traveler and give the date, time, and cities involved in the introduction.

1. Where does she check in?
2. What kind of baggage does she have?
3. Who carries her baggage?
4. Where does she go after the baggage check-in and what does she do there?
5. Where does she board?
6. Who puts her baggage up and where is it put?
7. Where will she sit?

1 From Hot Air to Jets

There are nineteen words from page 57 in this reading. Find and underline them.

Since early times, man has been interested in flight. In the 11th and 12th centuries, men wrote of their attempts to tie wings to their bodies in order to fly. In the 16th century, Leonardo da Vinci made careful studies of birds and then drew pictures of flying machines that went straight up into the air. They looked a lot like modern helicopters complete with rotors! The first real flight was in a hot air balloon in 1783. Later, balloons with propellers were invented, called blimps. In the 1890s an aircraft was developed that looked very much like an airplane, but without an engine. It was the first glider. The first manned flight in a propeller plane, however, was in 1903. This plane, developed and flown by the Wright Brothers, had all six essential parts of an airplane—a fuselage,

wings, tail, rudder, an engine, and wheels. Today these propeller planes seem very old-fashioned. Jet engines were soon to follow, however. Developed in the 18th century, the jet engine was first thought of for use on an aircraft in 1908. Now jet planes are very common.

Today, aircraft are commonly used for both sport and transportation. Hot air balloons are used as a form of recreation, and many daredevils enjoy the thrill of flying in hang gliders. It is not unusual to see business people in their own private jets. From busy airport terminal buildings, we see control towers directing runway traffic, huge cargo planes unloading at their cargo areas, and passenger planes on their way to huge hangars. Think how far air travel has come!

2 Just the Facts, Please

Now, on another sheet of paper, answer these questions.

1. How did man try to fly in the 11th and 12th centuries?

2. How did Leonardo da Vinci try to find out about the art of flying?

3. When was the first real flight? What kind of aircraft was it?

4. What is a blimp?

5. What is the main difference between a glider and an airplane?

6. What did the Wright Brothers do?

7. What are the six necessary parts of an airplane?

8. When were jet engines developed?

3 Research

Find out more about the six main parts of an airplane in a larger dictionary. Write an eight-sentence paragraph starting with this: *Most airplanes have six main parts.* Each of the next six sentences should mention a part and give a definition. Use words like *first*, *second*, etc. The eighth sentence will be your conclusion.

43 In Port page 58

1 That's Not True!

● 　Write five false sentences about the picture in the Dictionary.
○○ Exchange papers with a partner and correct the sentences.
　　There may be more than one way to correct them.

The ferry is at the dock.　　　*The ocean liner is at the dock.*

2 In Port

●
●○ Look at the picture to fill in these blanks. There may be more
　　than one good answer, and you may use a word more than once.

The people on the _____*pier*_____ gathered to watch the little _____ guide the

huge _____ past the _____ to the _____. Everyone

wondered what kind of cargo it was carrying. There were lots of _____ being lifted

out of the _____ of the ship. On the ship's _____, workers began to

hurry back and forth. After a while, the overhanging _____ started to lift the

containers off the ship.

　Nearby, an equally large _____ liner made ready to leave the _____.

Several people ran up the _____, and workers began to untie the

_____. As smoke rose from the _____, the _____ of the

ship slowly moved away from the _____. There were probably many passengers on

the ship because there were seven _____ on one side of the ship alone!

　In the distance, to the right of the _____, the crowd could see a long oil

_____. The _____, _____, and even the tanker, looked

tiny in contrast to the enormous ships in dock.

3 Idioms and Expressions

●
●● See if you can find out what these terms mean. Explain their
　　meanings on another sheet of paper.

1. shipshape　　2. in the same boat　　3. barge in

79

44 Pleasure Boating page 59

1 Analogies

Fill in the blanks with a word from page 59.

1. A paddle is to a canoe as an oar is to a _____.

2. A sail is to a sailboat as an outboard motor is to a _____.

2 Odd Man Out

Circle the one that doesn't belong and tell why.

1. boom (tow rope) mast   *It isn't part of a sailboat.*

2. rudder   centerboard   life preserver _____

3. windsurfer   water-skier   cabin cruiser _____

4. cabin cruiser   dinghy   motorboat _____

5. sailboat   canoe   kayak _____

3 Where Are They?

Read the following dialogues and decide where the speakers are.

1. A: Do we have any more gas in the boat?
   B: No! I hope we don't get stuck in the lake!
   On a motorboat.

2. A: Watch out for the boom!
   B: Thanks, I didn't see it coming!

   _____

3. A: Hello over there! That looks like fun.
   B: It is if you know how to paddle it
   correctly and not turn yourself over.

   _____

4. A: We're not going very fast!
   B: That's for sure! Give me the oars for a
   while!

   _____

5. A: We need to turn around pretty soon.
   B: OK, let's both paddle on one side for a
   while. That should turn us.

   _____

4 Student Interview

Choose a partner and interview each other about the types of water
sports you have done or would like to do. Report back to the class.

1 Girls' Names

As a class, decide how many of the flowers from pages 60–61 can be used as girls' names in English and also in your native languages. Can you think of any other flowers that can be used as names?

2 Matching

Find all the parts that belong to each plant. You will use some letters several times.

1. rose   *d, e, g, h, j, m, n,*

2. oak _____

3. daffodil _____

4. pine _____

5. cactus _____

6. wheat _____

a. bulb	f. cone	k. trunk
b. needle	g. petal	l. bark
c. acorn	h. bud	m. root
d. stem	i. grain	n. branch
e. thorn	j. leaf	o. twig

3 Sentence Construction

Write a sentence for each of the trees mentioned below. Use the information following each tree. Study the examples.

We get flowers from magnolia trees.
Magnolia trees give us beautiful, big, white, fragrant flowers.
We can make a beautiful bouquet from the magnolia tree.
Beautiful flowers grow on magnolia trees.

1. magnolia—beautiful, big, white, fragrant flowers

2. dogwood—lovely, white, four-petaled flowers

3. holly—bright red berries and shiny green leaves

4. pine—interesting cones and sharp needles

5. redwood, pine, and oak—building materials and furniture

6. maple—furniture

7. palm—coconuts

8. maple—syrup

9. willow—aspirin

10. eucalyptus—cough drops

4 Flower Names

 Underline all the flower names in the reading below. (There are fifteen.)

Did you ever wonder how flowers got their names? Many flowers were named after people. For example, the gardenia was named after Dr. Alex Garden, a botanist from Scotland. Dr. J.R. Poinsett, from the United States, developed the poinsettia, and the zinnia was named after a German professor of botany, Johann Zinn. Some were even named after gods, goddesses, and religious figures. The iris was named after the Greek goddess of the rainbow. Marigold originally meant Mary's gold.

Other flowers have names that simply describe them. For instance, the buttercup looks like a cup of butter, and the sunflower, of course, looks like the sun. In the English of long ago, daisy meant day's eye, and it certainly does look like an eye!

Still other flowers have names that were originally words in other languages. These words often describe the flower, too. A good example is the tulip. This comes from the Turkish word "tulbend," which means turban. It does look like a Turk's hat! Another one is the chrysanthemum, which comes from Greek words that mean "gold flower." Petunias get their name from a South American Indian word, "petun," which means tobacco. The petunia flower looks a lot like the tobacco flower.

Some flower names have to do with the use we have for it. Crocus comes from the Greek word for saffron, for instance, and we get this expensive spice from the stamens of the crocus! Other foreign names are just translations into English—lily and violet, from Latin, and hyacinth, from Greek.

It's hard to believe how much we can learn from the names of flowers!

5 A Bunch of Flower Questions

 Answer the questions with complete sentences.

1. Which flower looks like:

   a. a hat? _____

82

b. an eye? _____

c. the sun? _____

d. butter? _____

e. the tobacco flower? _____

2. Which flower was named after:

a. a German ? _____

b. a Scot? _____

c. its developer? _____

d. a goddess? _____

e. Mary? _____

3. From which flower do we get a very expensive spice? _____

6 Student Composition

Look at the reading in exercise 4 and the information about trees in exercise 3. Write an article of your own entitled "Gifts From Trees." Use the following introduction and conclusion.

Introduction: *Did you ever think about how many ways we use trees?*
Conclusion: *It's amazing how many things we get from trees.*

Divide your article into four paragraphs.

Paragraph one —   Write about #1–4 in exercise 3 (what decorative things we get from trees).

Paragraph two —   Write about #5–6 (what good wood we get from trees).

Paragraph three — Write about #7–8 (the foods we get from trees).

Paragraph four —   Write about #9–10 (the drugs made from trees).

46 Simple Animals page 62

1 Fitting Descriptions

● Write down the name of the animal that is being described.
○○

1. You can almost see through it.   *jellyfish*

2. It's gray in color and good to eat. _____

3. It's large, has eight tentacles, and shoots out "ink." _____

4. It has a shell, many legs, and is good to eat. _____

5. It has a shell and moves very slowly across the ground. _____

6. Sometimes you can find pearls in this. _____

7. It has two claws and its tail is good to eat. _____

8. Fishermen love to put these on their hooks. _____

9. It has five points. _____

10. It has a pretty, fan-shaped shell. _____

2 Naming Exercise

● Name the simple animals that have these characteristics. Put
●○ your answers into sentence form. The number in parentheses
tells you how many animals you will find like this on page 62.

1. shells (7)

   *The lobster, shrimp, crab, mussel, oyster,
   scallop, and snail have shells.*

2. claws (2)

3. legs (3)

4. antennas (4)

5. tentacles (3)

6. shells/no antennas (4)

7. no shell/antennas (1)

8. shells/antennas (3)

9. two claws/antennas (1)

10. one claw/no antennas (1)

11. no antennas/no claws/no tentacles/no shell (2)

3 Seafood Tastes

●● Get together with a partner and interview each other about
●● what kind of seafood each of you particularly like and dislike.
Take notes and write a one-paragraph report. Read it to the class.

84

47 Insects page 63

1 Bug Problems

Many people dislike having insects and spiders around them. They buy insecticides to get rid of them. Read these labels to decide which bug the insecticide will best kill. Write your answers on another sheet of paper.

1. Spray monthly. Keep them from eating all the wooden parts of your house!
2. Hang these strips in your closet to protect your woolen clothes.
3. Apply the powder along the baseboards in your kitchen and bathroom.
4. Spray the nest directly from at least 12 feet and leave immediately.
5. Spray the garden area about half an hour before having your party.
6. Put these buttons in kitchen cabinets—especially near sugar and sweets.
7. Spray garbage cans weekly to prevent attracting them.

2 The Collector

Although some people want to get rid of bugs, others like to collect them! Read the following essay and answer the questions in complete sentences on another sheet of paper.

Marcia is a biology teacher who collects insects and spiders. She has a beautiful collection of butterflies and moths. She loves to show her students how the most beautiful butterflies and moths come from cocoons made by the ugliest caterpillars. Last summer, Marcia added some hard-to-find beetles and dragonflies to her collection. They are not like fireflies, which light up to show you where they are, or crickets, which make noise! This year she wants to find some large mantises. She'll put one in her collection and the rest in her yard to keep garden pests away.

It seems that some insects do not like to be collected, however. Last week two wasps and a bee stung her! Mosquitos and flies don't like her either! Although some insects, like the grasshopper, look dangerous, they aren't. A few insects, on the other hand, can be really dangerous. When Marcia hunts scorpions, centipedes, and certain spiders, she is extremely careful not to allow them to sting or bite her! Actually, spiders, scorpions, and centipedes are not insects because they have more than six legs. Most people don't worry about the difference, though, and call everything she collects a bug!

1. How many legs does an insect have?
2. Which bugs are not insects?
3. Which insect is good in the garden?
4. Which bugs can be dangerous?
5. What does she like to show her class?
6. What is the common word for what Marcia collects?
7. Which insects are easy to find and why?

48 Birds page 64

1 Groupings

There are many ways to group birds. On another sheet of paper, list birds from page 64 under each of the categories. You may use a bird on several lists.

Birds for Food   Pets   Beautiful Birds   Birds of Prey

2 All Wrong

The following statements are not correct. Correct them by drawing a line through the name of the bird and writing the correct bird's name on the line. There may be more than one correct answer, and you may use some birds more than once.

1. The flamingo lives in a very cold place.   *penguin*

2. The parakeet is good to eat.   _____

3. A swan can talk.   _____

4. The hummingbird is the largest living bird.   _____

5. The crow has a long neck.   _____

6. The sparrow has a beautiful tail.   _____

7. The crow is pink.   _____

8. The pigeon is a very fast runner.   _____

9. The robin makes holes in wood.   _____

10. The stork is all red.   _____

3 Corrections

Look at the sentences in exercise 2 again. Now correct them on the lines below. The first two are done. Notice how the two examples are different. Your teacher will help you see the difference.

1. *The flamingo doesn't live in a very cold place, but the penguin does.*

2. *The parakeet isn't good to eat, but a chicken is.*

86

3. _____

4. _____

5. _____

6. _____

7. _____

8. _____

9. _____

10. _____

4 Use Your Imagination

Imagine that you could be any bird that you wanted to be.
Write a paragraph explaining why you would like to be that
bird, and what the advantages would be. After that, choose a
bird that you know you would not want to be and explain why.

5 Idioms and Expressions

With the help of a partner, try to find out what the following
phrases mean and use them in sentences. Read your sentences
to the class.

1. a bird in the hand is worth two in the bush _____

2. cook one's goose _____

3. the early bird catches the worm _____

4. nest egg _____

5. kill two birds with one stone _____

6. water off a duck's back _____

7. a wild goose chase _____

49 Fish and Reptiles page 65

1 Comparisons

Answer these questions on another sheet of paper. Follow the example.

A. Which is more dangerous:

1. a trout or a shark? *A shark is more dangerous.*

2. a sea horse or a stingray?

3. alligators or frogs?

4. turtles or salamanders?

B. Which is the most dangerous:

1. a garter snake, a rattlesnake, or a cobra?

2. iguanas, turtles, or alligators?

2 At the Aquarium

Read the following comments made by children on a trip to the zoo aquarium. Decide which underwater animals they are talking about.

1. It looks like a flying sheet with a tail!   *It must be a stingray.*

2. It has the longest nose I've ever seen!   _____

3. It looks like a snake, but it's not!   _____

4. Look at the cute little horse!   _____

5. Its teeth look very sharp!   _____

6. That fish has spots!   _____

3 Now You Try It!

On another sheet of paper, write six comments that the children might make as they look at the reptiles and amphibians. After you've finished, exchange papers with a partner and write answers to each other's questions.

4 Snakes and Sharks

Many people are afraid of snakes and sharks, perhaps because of all the horrible things they've seen in movies. Write a paragraph about your feelings toward either one. Explain why you feel the way you do.

50 Mammals pages 66–69

1 Comparison Riddles

Solve the riddles. Write the answers in the blanks.

1. It has stripes and looks like a horse.   *zebra*

2. It has spots and looks like a cat.   _____

3. It has a horn in the middle of its nose and
   looks like a hippopotamus.   _____

4. It's wild and looks like a dog.   _____

5. It's black and white and looks like a bear.   _____

6. It's very big and looks like a fish.   _____

2 Um, Um, Good!

Animals that people consider to be good to eat differ from place
to place. On another sheet of paper, make a list of animals that
may be eaten in your native country, but are not commonly
eaten where you live now. Compare your list with those of
your classmates.

3 More Comparisons

Here are some common expressions in English that compare
people's actions to animals. Write a plus if it's a positive thing to
say about someone and a minus if it's not. Then write
sentences using these expressions. Share your sentences with
the class.

_____ 1. eats like a horse   _____ 7. quick as a rabbit

_____ 2. smells like a skunk   _____ 8. blind as a bat

_____ 3. gentle as a lamb   _____ 9. busy as a beaver

_____ 4. big as a whale   _____ 10. fat as a hog

_____ 5. sly as a fox   _____ 11. quiet as a mouse

_____ 6. brave as a lion

4 Other Comparisons

There are many other comparisons between people and animals in English. You may know some in your own language. You might even be able to invent some! Write comparisons like the ones above. Compare them to ones your classmates write.

5 Places of Origin

Look at these maps that show where various animals live. Then fill in the blanks in the reading on the opposite page.

Australia	Africa	North America	Sumatra/Borneo	China	South America

Some animals of the world can be found in special places only. For example, if you want to see a

_____, a cousin to the camel, you must travel to the Andes in South America. On

the other hand, if you are interested in the _____ or the _____,

Australia is the place for you. Many animal lovers tour Africa to find _____,

_ _____, _____, _____, and _____. And of

those, the _____ is nearly extinct. North America is the only place to find the

American __ _____, or what some people call the buffalo. They cannot be found in the

wild anymore, and are only found on special reserves. The nearly extinct _____ bear

is also native to North America, as are the smaller animals like the _ _____,

_____, _____, _____, and _____. Sumatra

and Borneo are the places to go to find the _____, and the bear-like

_ _____ is only seen in China. If you'd like to see these unusual animals and don't

have the money to explore the world, try visiting your local zoo!

6 Which Are You?

Choose an animal from pages 66–69 that seems to be most like
you. Write a paragraph about how you and this animal are
alike. Then, in another paragraph, write about an animal that
seems to have the opposite characteristics of you.

51 Map of the World pages 70–71

1 Map Search

Fill in the blanks with words from pages 70–71.

1. The continent north of Africa is _____.

2. The _____ Sea is southeast of the Rub' Al Khali Desert.

3. The desert in south central Asia is the _____ _____ Desert.

4. The large bay in the northeast part of North America is the _____ Bay.

5. The mountains running in a north-south direction on the west coast of South America are the

   _____.

6. The huge river that runs in a north-south direction in Africa is the _____.

7. The two deserts in the western part of North America are the _____ and the

   _____.

8. The _____ Sea is northeast of the Mediterranean Sea.

9. The _____ _____ and _____ Mountains run north

   and south along the western part of North America.

10. The three seas north of Europe and Asia are the _____ Sea, the

    _____ Sea, and the _____ Sea.

11. The _____ _____ Desert is in northwest Australia.

12. The _____ River runs in a north-south direction in central North America.

2 Descriptions of Home

On another sheet of paper, give a geographic description of where you were born and where you live now. Give details about the bodies of water, rivers, mountains, and deserts that are nearby.

3 Extremes

Read the following paragraph. On another sheet of paper, write questions and answers based on the words that come after it.

Each of the continents of the world is extraordinary in some way. For instance, Asia has the largest land mass of 16,988,000 square miles. It also has the highest mountain range—the Himalayas, where Mount Everest stands 29,028 feet tall. Africa has the longest river, the Nile, measuring 4,145 miles long. North America lies between the two largest oceans. The Pacific holds 23.9% of the world's water, while the Atlantic has 46% of the world's water. North America also has the Mississippi, the third longest river. South America has the driest spot in the world, the Atacama desert. It's even drier than the Sahara in Africa. In addition, South America has the world's second longest river, the Amazon. Eastern Europe has the largest lake. Although it is called a sea because it is so large (143,550 square miles), the Caspian Sea is really a lake. Vostok, Antarctica, is the coldest spot on earth, with a recorded temperature of -127°F in 1960. Australia is said to have the fewest people (.3% of the world's population), even though Antarctica has even fewer because, comparatively speaking, it is not populated at all!

1. larger/Asia or Africa?

2. largest continent?

3. higher/Himalayas or Alps?

4. Caspian/lake or sea?

5. lowest temperature?

6. Sahara/driest?

7. Asia/square miles?

8. largest ocean?

9. colder/Antarctica or North America?

10. percentage people/Australia?

4 World Travel

Using the map, write a paragraph about the route you last took (by plane, car, ship, or train) from your native country to where you now live. Mention the bodies of water, land masses, mountains, deserts, etc. that you passed, and in which directions you were traveling. Was this the shortest route? Why did you take this route?

52 The United States of America pages 72–73

1 The States

Look at the picture in the Dictionary and answer the following questions on another sheet of paper.

1. Which four states meet at one central point?

2. What are the three states south of Tennessee?

3. Which is the state farthest to the west?

4. Which state is the most northeastern?

5. Which state is the most southeastern?

6. Which state is the most northwestern?

7. Which two pairs of states have a north and a south in their names?

2 Cities

The ten largest U.S. cities are shown as dots on this map. Read the following descriptions and number the cities 1–10.

1. New York is the largest U.S. city, and it's in New York State.

2. Chicago is at the southern end of Lake Michigan in the state of Illinois.

3. Los Angeles is in southern California on the Pacific coast.

4. Philadelphia is in southeastern Pennsylvania.

5. Houston is in southeastern Texas near the Gulf of Mexico.

6. Detroit is in the state of Michigan near Lake Erie and Lake Huron.

7. San Diego is also in southern California, not far from Mexico.

8. San Antonio is another city in Texas, this time in the central part of southern Texas.

9. Phoenix is in south central Arizona.

10. Honolulu is on one of the Hawaiian islands.

3 National Parks

The United States has 38 national parks. Put the following twelve parks on the previous map by marking them with an "x" and numbering them 11–22.

11. Yellowstone was the first national park. It was established in 1872. It's where Idaho, Wyoming, and Montana meet.

12. Wind Cave National Park is in the Black Hills of southwestern South Dakota.

13. Rocky Mountain National Park is in the Rocky Mountains, of course, in northwestern Colorado.

14. The Great Smoky Mountain National Park belongs to two states—North Carolina and Tennessee. It's about halfway down their shared border.

15. Isle Royale is a big island in Lake Superior that belongs to the state of Michigan.

16. Big Bend is on the Rio Grande River in Texas where the river makes a very big bend.

17. Shenandoah National Park is in the Blue Ridge Mountains of northern Virginia.

18. Midway along the coast of Maine is the beautiful Acadia National Park.

19. Yosemite is in the Sierra Nevada Mountains in east central California.

20. Southern Florida has a beautiful national park called The Everglades.

21. Glacier is another park in the Rocky Mountains in northwestern Montana.

22. The Grand Canyon is on the Colorado River in northern Arizona.

4 USA Tour

Plan a trip to visit all the places you would most like to see in the United States. On another sheet of paper, describe your trip by telling what cities, parks, and natural features you would travel to and why.

53 The Universe page 74

1 Space Spaces

● Fill in the blanks with words from page 74.
○○

1. The _____ moon is round.

2. The _____ moon is completely dark.

3. The Big Dipper is a _____.

4. Watch the stars through a _____.

5. A _____ has a tail.

6. Some _____s fall to earth.

7. In a _____ eclipse, we cannot see the sun.

2 Describing Our Solar System

● Look at the picture and put the following groups of sentences
●○ into logical order. The first one is done in each paragraph.

Paragraph 1

_____ It is about three-fifths of the way from the center of the galaxy.

___1___ Our sun is only one of 100 billion stars grouped together in our galaxy.

_____ Nine planets orbit this star. The closer ones orbit faster than the farther ones.

Paragraph 2

_____ After Venus comes our own Earth.

_____ Venus hides its hot surface under clouds.

_____ The second planet is Venus, where temperatures may reach 900° F.

_____ The reflection from the clouds makes Venus shine even brighter than some stars.

___1___ Mercury, the closest planet to the Sun, makes its orbit in only 88 days.

Paragraph 3

_____ Farther out from the largest planet is Saturn, with its colorful rings.

_____ Between Mars and the next planet, Jupiter, there is a ring of about 2,000 asteroids.

___1___ Beyond the Earth comes Mars, which is covered with craters, or surface holes.

_____ Jupiter, the largest planet, spins at a speed of 28,000 miles per hour.

_____ Beyond the planets, there are some comets with unmeasured orbits.

_____ The last planets are icy Uranus, green Neptune, and the very distant Pluto, which is almost three billion miles away.

3 Quick Quiz

Answer the following questions based on the information in exercise 2.

1. Which planet orbits faster—Mercury or Pluto?

_____

2. The asteroids orbit between which two planets?

_____

3. What bodies orbit even beyond Pluto?

_____

4. Why is it difficult to see Venus's surface?

_____

5. Why is Venus so bright in the sky?

_____

54 The Space Program page 75

1 Matching

●
○○ Scientists now have many ways to get important information.
Which tool would you use to get the following information?

_____ 1. a close-up picture of Saturn's rings

_____ 2. a photograph of clouds covering the Earth

_____ 3. news from around the world

_____ 4. samples of the Moon's surface

a. lunar module

b. space probe

c. space station

d. communication satellite

2 A Job in Space

●
●○ Read the following paragraphs and fill in the blanks.

Three hours before takeoff, the _____ checked to see that everything was all right

in their _____ shuttle. All of the _____ were looking forward to

blastoff. Their job in space was to dock with a _____ satellite to repair it. Satellites

like these were very important to fast global communication.

The huge _____ fired, and the space _____ rose from the

_____ into the air. In about six minutes the craft was traveling 15 times the speed of

sound. The _____ _____ that the astronauts wore kept them from

feeling sick. At 690 miles up, the spacecraft went into orbit.

The next day the crew successfully docked with the satellite. They opened the

_____ bay doors and spent the next few hours repairing the satellite. When they

were finished, they dropped back to Earth.

The crowd watched the spacecraft open and the astronauts come out. They were happy to be

home because their _____ _____ inside the spacecraft had been very

small.

3 Dictionary Work

Words often have more than one meaning. Read the definitions for these words and circle the one that refers to the space program.

1. bay
   a) a reddish-brown color
   b) any compartment in the fuselage of an aircraft
   c) an inlet of the sea
   d) to bark continuously like a dog

2. rocket
   a) a bomb or missile, used as a weapon
   b) a firework used to display bright colors in the sky
   c) a jet used to send up a vehicle

3. satellite
   a) a natural body in space that orbits another body—like the Moon orbits the Earth
   b) a follower
   c) a man-made object or vehicle made to orbit a body in space

4. deck
   a) a platform on a ship
   b) a pack of playing cards
   c) a flat-floored, roofless structure attached to a house

1 No Talking, Please!

What items on page 76 are the students in the following dialogues talking about or using?

A: I made a mistake! 　　B: Here, take this and change your answer!

1. *eraser*

A: Do you have any extra discs? 　　B: No, ask the teacher.

2. _____

A: I'm out of ink! 　　B: Here, borrow mine!

3. _____

A: The principal sure makes a lot of announcements! 　　B: She sure does!

4. _____

A: Where's your lunch? 　　B: It's out in the hall.

5. _____

A: Can everyone see the picture? 　　B: No, let's turn the lights off.

6. _____

A: It won't stay up on the board! 　　B: Here, tack it up!

7. _____

2 Assignments

The teacher asked the students to do the following assignments. Fill in the blanks to tell what the students did. You may use a word more than once.

1. "Please answer the questions on page 46 in ink and hand in at 3:00."

   The _____s got out their _____s and answered the questions on

   _____ paper with _____ _____ _____s.

2. "With sharp pencils, connect the points on the graph and glue the graph into your notebooks."

   After the _____s got out _____ __ _____s to prepare

   their pencils, they connected the points on their papers with _____s. Then they

   used _____ and _____es to glue the graphs into their

   _____ notebooks.

3. "Jerry, erase the writing on the board and put your own problem up."

   Jerry went up to the _____. He got an _____ from another student

   and cleaned the board. Then he got a piece of _____ _____ from the __ _____

   _____ and put up his problem.

4. "John will project his map up here while the rest of you finish your own maps and tack them

   to the board."

   John used the _____ _____ to project his map on the screen. The

   rest of the _____s got out their _____s to correct their maps. The

   _____ __ gave each child a _____ so that he could tack his corrected

   map to the _____ board.

3 A Busy Day

Make a list of all of the classroom tools you have used so far today. Write a paragraph about what you have done. Include all of the words on your list.

56 School Verbs page 77

1 General School Rules

Fill in the blanks with verbs from page 77. There may be more than one good answer, and you may use a word more than once.

1. Never _____ pictures on your desks!

2. Never _____ the classroom unless you _____ your hand!

3. _____ down the halls—never run!

4. Don't _____ carelessly on the chalkboard!

5. _____ to the teacher's instructions!

6. _____ the classroom quietly.

7. Always _____ your name in your notebooks.

8. _____ the chalkboards before going home.

9. Always _____ the directions in your textbooks!

10. Remember to _____ your locker doors!

11. Don't _____ things on the teacher's desk!

12. Never _____ the pages of your textbooks!

13. Don't _____ the typewriter unless you know how to _____!

14. Never let the flag _____ the floor!

2 Classy Sentences

Use all the words in each group in a single sentence.

1. teacher/close/textbooks/listen/loudspeaker

2. student/type/computer

3. raise/hand/read/textbook

4. draw/chalkboard/chalk/chalk tray

3 Descriptive Sentences

Look at the pictures. Write one sentence to describe what is happening in each picture. Try to use a verb from page 77 and a noun from page **76** in each one.

1 True or False

Some of the following sentences are true and some aren't.
Mark true (T) or false (F).

_____ 1. A flask and a beaker are both containers.
_____ 2. Test tubes come in a dissection kit.
_____ 3. A Bunsen burner produces a flame.
_____ 4. Use a funnel to pick things up.
_____ 5. To use a scale, you need a petri dish.
_____ 6. Look through a microscope at something on a prism.
_____ 7. Use safety glasses to make things look bigger.
_____ 8. Use a clamp on a magnet.
_____ 9. You can put stoppers in test tubes.
_____ 10. Use a pipette to bring gas to a Bunsen burner.
_____ 11. Use a timer to pick something up.
_____ 12. Use graph paper to measure liquids.

2 The Right Way

On another sheet of paper, correct all the false sentences from exercise 1.
There may be more than one way to make the sentences right.

3 An Experiment With Sugar

The lines of the following experiment are not given in the
correct order. Order them by numbering 1, 2, 3, etc. Do each
paragraph separately. The first lines are marked.

_____ burner and set the flame low. Set the timer for five minutes so that you
_____ burner, and place a wire mesh screen over the ring. At the same time,
___1___ Connect a Bunsen burner to a gas line with some rubber tubing. Place the
_____ do not forget your experiment. Place a glass slide across the beaker.
_____ sugar in a beaker. Set the beaker on top of the mesh. Light the Bunsen
_____ burner on a ring stand. Set the clamp and ring a few inches above the
_____ weigh out five grams of sugar, using the weights and the scale. Put the

_____ and taste it. Does it taste sweet? No, it doesn't! Although we have
_____ and shake. Remove a little water from the test tube with an eye dropper
_____ and taste a drop to make sure it is water. It seems, then, that sugar is
_____ again to make sugar!
___1___ Watch the sugar melt and form black carbon. Also, watch the glass slide.
_____ made up of carbon and water (hydrogen and oxygen). Remove the beaker
_____ separated sugar into its three parts, we cannot mix those parts together
_____ with tongs, and scrape some of the carbon into a test tube. Add water
_____ Drops of water will form on the slide. Remove the slide with tweezers,

1 Follow Directions

Use a pencil, ruler, and compass and follow the directions below.

1. Draw a circle around the square.

2. Draw an oval around the cylinder.

3. Label the half-pie brown, the third of a pie red, and the quarter-pie blue.

4. Draw another parallel line below the two shown.

5. Draw another radius from the center of the circle.

6. Draw a rectangle around the pyramid.

7. Connect the perpendicular lines.

8. Make the curve longer so that it touches the straight line.

9. Label the obtuse angle red, the right angle blue, and the acute angle yellow.

10. Draw a diagonal in the square.

11. Write 12 inches as the depth of the shelves, 3 feet as the height, and 2½ feet as the width.

12. Show the length of the rope as 8 inches.

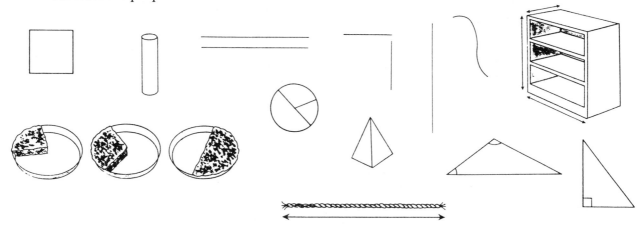

2 Definitions

Write a definition for each of the following words. Use as many other words from page 79 as possible. Look at the example.

1. triangle   *This figure has three sides and three angles.*

2. rectangle   3. square   4. circle   5. cube   6. pyramid

3 Find One!

With a partner, find as many examples of the words from page 79 as you can in your classroom. Compare the number of examples you found with the number found by your classmates.

59 Energy page 80

1 U.S. Energy

● Look at the circle graph and write sentences describing the
○○ types of energy used in the United States.

31.5 percent of our energy comes from oil.

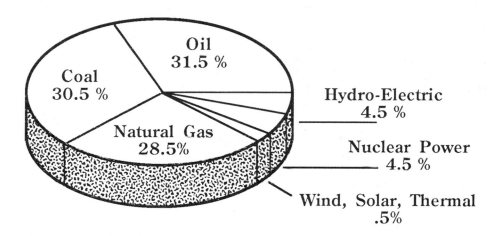

2 Energy

● Read the paragraphs. Answer the questions following it on
●○ another sheet of paper.

The sun is the source of all our energy. Look at the graph to see the major forms of energy in the world, and how much of our total energy we get from each of these forms in the United States. Although it's obvious that solar power comes from the sun, is it possible that all the other energy forms depend upon the sun, too?

Oil, the most commonly used U.S. fuel, was once the plants and animals of the Earth's oceans. The sun was necessary for them to live. Today we find oil deep in the Earth and dig oil wells to pump the oil out. Huge refineries clean it, and power stations burn it so that electrical generators can transform the heat into electricity.

Coal and natural gas are also products of once-living plants and animals—in this case, land plants and animals. While we dig coal mines to get coal out of the Earth, we pipe out natural gas. Again, power plants are necessary to make electricity. Nuclear reactors, on the other hand, generate electricity from uranium, a naturally-found material on Earth.

The sun heats the Earth unevenly, so some air warms up quickly, while some stays cool. Warm air rises, and when it does cooler air moves in to fill the space the warm air left behind. We call this constant movement of air the wind. Windmills use the energy of the wind to generate electricity.

The sun also causes water to evaporate from the oceans and fall as rain on the land. Rivers develop, which then form waterfalls. Dams generate hydroelectric power from these waterfalls.

In its center, our Earth is very, very hot. Water underground can be heated to produce steam. Geysers are places where this steam and water escape above ground in a giant spray. Man can also use this thermal energy as a power source.

So, directly or indirectly, the sun is the source of almost all our energy!

1. What is the third most important fuel in the United States?

2. What three forms of energy were once living things? How do they differ?

3. What do refineries do?

4. How do we get electricity from oil, gas, and coal?

5. What three forms of energy are not commonly used in the United States?

6. What do you think thermal energy is?

7. What do you think hydroelectric power is?

3 Energy Problems

What is the main source of energy in your native country? Where do you get this fuel? Does it cause pollution problems? Write a paragraph about energy problems at home.

60 Farming and Ranching page 81

1 Picture Puzzle

Look at the pictures in the Dictionary and then answer the following questions in complete sentences on another sheet of paper.

On the Dairy Farm:

1. What two kinds of animals are in the picture?

2. What is between the barn and the farmhouse?

3. What is the fenced-in area near the orchard?

4. What's in an orchard?

On the Wheat Farm:

1. What is standing up against the barn?

2. What three kinds of animals are in the barnyard?

3. What's parked in the barn?

On the Ranch:

1. What's the horse drinking from?

2. What are the cowboy and cowgirl herding?

2 Farm Problems

Make up sentences to complete these farm/ranch dialogues. Use as many of the words from page 81 as possible.

1. Farmer #1: The birds are getting all my wheat!

Farmer #2: _____

Farmer #1: That's a good idea! I'll get one tomorrow!

2. Farmer #1: All my animals got out of the barnyard last night!

Farmer #2: _____

Farmer #1: I know. I'll have to fix it today.

3. Farmer #1: I hope I have enough hay to last through the year!

Farmer #2: _____

Farmer #1: I have almost five hundred in the barn.

3 Your Own Experience

Have you ever spent any time on a farm or a ranch? Did it look like the ones in the pictures? On another sheet of paper, tell what kind of farm/ranch it was, where it was, and what it looked like.

1 Strip Stories

Look at the following strip stories and write the words from page 82 that you see in the pictures on the lines below.

1.

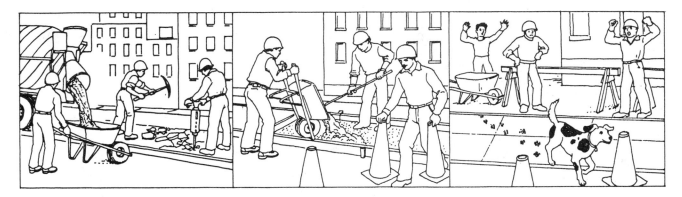

_____ _____ _____

2.

_____ _____ _____

2 Group Work

Work with two other students. Each of you take one picture in each of the strip stories and describe it to the rest of the group. Describe what the workers are wearing, as well as what they are doing. Be ready as a group to present each strip story to the class.

3 On Your Own

Write down a description of each strip story in detail. Read it to the class.

62 An Office page 83

1 A Day's Work

What does each person in an office do? Mention at least three activities that each office worker would take care of every day.

1. manager   *supervises other workers*
2. switchboard operator   3. typist   4. secretary   5. file clerk

2 What's the Subject?

Read the following quotes and decide which item from page 83 the person is talking about.

1. "There are a lot of telephone calls coming in. Where is she?"   _____

2. "We'll have to take some file folders out. I can't get any more folders to fit in!"   _____

3. "If you can't find one that works, use paper clips."   _____

4. "She's not in the office today, but I can let you speak to her secretary if you'd like."   _____

5. "It's sure a lot easier and faster to use than a typewriter!"   _____

6. "There are several addressed to you in the in-box."   _____

3 Step by Step

Put these office situations into a logical order.

_____ The typist gives the computer printout to the manager.

_____ The secretary writes the information on a legal pad.

_____ The secretary gives the information to the typist, who puts it on a word processor.

_____ The manager tells the secretary some information.

_____ She then copies the paper on the photocopier.

_____ The secretary types a paper on the typewriter.

_____ The file clerk files the stapled papers in the file cabinet.

_____ She uses the stapler to add the copy to other papers.

1 Information, Please

● Whom would you call if you needed:
○○

1. your house cleaned? _____

2. bread? _____

3. a new house? _____

4. eyeglasses? _____

5. vegetables? _____

6. your hair cut? _____

7. your lights fixed? _____

8. flowers? _____

9. your water pipes fixed? _____

10. meat for dinner? _____

2 Help Wanted

● Read the following parts of want ads. Decide who should
○○ answer the ad. There may be more than one good answer.

MUST HAVE FIVE OR MORE YEARS EXPERIENCE CUTTING AND SETTING STONES.

Must work fast and be able to finish a three-room apartment in a day.

Garage needs a brake specialist.

DEPARTMENT STORE NEEDS AN EXPERT IN FITTING MEN'S SUITS.

1. _____   2. _____   3. _____   4. _____

HOMEOWNER SEARCHING FOR SOMEONE TO CUT GRASS AND TRIM BUSHES.

SMALL AGENCY NEEDS SOMEONE TO RESERVE SUMMER TOURS.

Wanted: Elementary school looking for someone to clean and maintain building.

WORKER NEEDED FOR THE LATE SHIFT ON AN ASSEMBLY LINE

5. _____   6. _____   7. _____   8. _____

3 Good Qualifications

● You need certain qualifications to work at most jobs. Choose
●○ one (or more) of the occupations from pages 84, 85, and 86 to
match the following qualifications.

1. honest _____

2. a good mathematician _____

3. good language skills _____

4. artistic _____

5. good looking _____

6. a pleasant speaking voice _____

7. college graduate _____

8. fast moving _____

4 Quotes

Read the following quotes by the professionals on page 86.
Decide who is speaking.

1. "I like traveling with news reporters and being a part of the TV world."

   _____

2. "I've worked at this job for fifteen years and have never had to draw my gun."

   _____

3. "Today will be slightly cloudy with the wind coming from the west."

   _____

4. "Sign the check on the back, sir. Do you want it in tens or twenties?"

   _____

5. "The next record is a new one by the Rocking Horses."

   _____

6. "The blueprints show five windows on the ground floor."

   _____

7. "This year big pockets, longer dresses, and skirts will be popular."

   _____

5 Your Job

What is your profession or occupation? In a few sentences, describe what you do and why you enjoy (or don't enjoy) your job. If you are a full-time student, describe the kind of job you would like to have in the future.

6 Take Out an Ad!

On another sheet of paper, write some want ads of your own for the following people:

| pharmacist | carpenter | locksmith | delivery boy |
| reporter | doorman | photographer | computer programmer |

64 Neighborhood Parks page 87

1 Park Rules

There must be rules at the park so everyone can have fun safely. Complete these park rules by filling in the blanks with words from page 87.

1. Don't throw litter in the _____. The ducks might swallow it. Throw it in the

   _____ _____.

2. Don't walk behind the _____. You may get hit.

3. Don't play around when you're getting a drink at the _____ _____.

4. Don't throw sand when you're in the _____. It may get in someone's eyes.

5. Don't jog in the _____ _____; the riders may run into you.

6. Don't go down the _____ backward; it's dangerous.

2 Dictionary Work

Choose a word from page 87 to match the following definitions.

1. a long seat for two or more persons _____

2. a person who sells _____

3. a place where music is performed outdoors _____

4. a piece of playground equipment made up of a balanced board that goes up and down _____

5. a piece of playground equipment made up of horizontal and vertical bars _____

6. a park ride with seats in the form of animals that goes round and round _____

7. a trail for horseback riding _____

3 The Babysitter

Imagine that you are responsible for a seven-year-old child for three hours. The child wants to go to the park. On a separate sheet of paper, explain how you would keep the child busy at the park.

65 Outdoor Activities pages 88–89

1 Outdoor Fun

Read the following descriptions of people about to spend the weekend outdoors. Then choose the best activity for each one.

A. camping   B. mountain climbing   C. rafting   D. fishing   E. hiking

_____ 1. Jay and Sherry love excitement, action, and waterfalls.

_____ 2. The Morris brothers enjoy lazy afternoons on a sunny stream, baiting a hook.

_____ 3. The Davis family likes to sleep in tents in the woods.

_____ 4. Mike and Susan prefer getting out their backpacks and walking in the fresh air.

_____ 5. Mary and Jane are in good physical condition and enjoy the excitement of climbing to the tops of high peaks.

2 Word Scramble

The people in exercise 1 went on their weekend trips, but forgot necessary items. Unscramble the following sentences to find out what they forgot.

1. their Jane forgot Mary ropes and and harnesses

2. brought The family should camp have Davis their stove

3. brothers couldn't Morris find their The waders

4. Susan have didn't shorts and their Mike hiking

5. left and jackets Sherry their Jay life home at

3 Positives and Negatives

Forgetting items is not all that went wrong with the people in exercise 1. However, some things went well, too. Put a plus or a minus in front of these statements to show whether it is a good point or a bad point.

_____ 1. The stream was full of big fish and the brothers caught a lot.
_____ 2. Mary and Jane saw a splendid view from the mountain peak.
_____ 3. Rain came through the hole in the Davis's tent.
_____ 4. Mary's lifeline broke.

_____ 5. The biggest fish took the bait and the hook, too.
_____ 6. Ants got into the Davis's picnic basket.
_____ 7. Going over the rapids, Jay fell out of the raft.
_____ 8. The grill cooked the fish perfectly.
_____ 9. There were no dangerous waterfalls for the raft to go over.
_____ 10. The sleeping bags were warm and comfortable.

4 Yellowstone National Park

Read the following article. On another sheet of paper, ask questions about the article using the words that follow it. Have a partner answer your questions.

Yellowstone National Park, the first national park in the United States, was established in 1872. It offers a wide variety of recreation.

Yellowstone lies on a wide plateau in the Rocky Mountains of Wyoming, Montana, and Idaho. For those who like scenic hiking, it has deep canyons and overlooking cliffs. The Grand Canyon of the Yellowstone is a sight to see, and hikers particularly like the South Rim Trail along the Canyon. Backpackers are attracted to the hundreds of trails, and for those who enjoy mountain climbing, high mountains, such as Joseph Peak (10,497 feet high) and Parker Peak (10,203 feet high), surround the plateau.

Rafters come to the raging rivers and streams for excitement, and many fishermen are found on the large lakes and rivers. In fact, the fishing is so good that they've even named a bridge Fishing Bridge. Photographers snap thousands of pictures of the beautiful waterfalls, like the Upper Falls of the Yellowstone River, which is 109 feet tall. Thousands of tourists camp in the woods every summer and more come just to sightsee and picnic.

In order to make your trip more enjoyable, you should contact a park ranger after getting there. He or she can tell you the rules and how to make the most of your trip. For instance, campfires are allowed in camping areas only, and you may not picnic outside of picnic areas. Register before going on any backpacking or hiking trips, and always carry a compass. By cooperating with the rangers, you can help make sure that people will always be able to enjoy the wonders of Yellowstone.

1. hiking

   What should you do before hiking in Yellowstone?

2. peak   4. canyon   6. campfire   8. stream   10. park ranger

3. waterfall   5. plateau   7. picnic   9. cliffs

114

66 At the Beach pages 90–91

1 Good Advice

Match these statements with the results.

_____ 1. They don't want to get a sunburn.   a. Call the lifeguard.

_____ 2. The sand is hot!   b. Play with the Frisbee.

_____ 3. The waves are big.   c. Go back to the motel.

_____ 4. The swimmer is going out too far.   d. Stand on the beach towel.

_____ 5. They want some exercise.   e. Put on some suntan lotion.

_____ 6. It's raining.   f. Get out the surfboard!

2 The Perfect Ending

Write your own advice by completing these sentences. Use the given word.

1. (whistle) Some swimmers were too close to some dangerous rocks, so _____

_____

2. (life preserver) The lifeboat came near the drowning swimmer and _____

_____

3. (cooler) The kids were thirsty, so _____

_____

4. (mask and snorkel) They wanted to see some colorful fish, so _____

_____

5. (air mattress) The tube had a hole in it, so _____

_____

6. (refreshment stand) The entire family was hungry, so _____

_____

7. (binoculars) She saw an interesting bird on the beach, so _____

_____

8. (wave) The children built a beautiful sandcastle, but _____

_____

9. (sunglasses) The sun was very bright, so _____

10. (kite) The wind was blowing hard, so _____

3 Survey

Work with another student. Ask each other the following questions.
Write down the answers and report your findings to the class.

1. Do you like the beach? If so, why? If not, why not?

2. Have you ever been sunburned? If so, what was the worst time?

3. Have you ever lived near a beach? If so, where? Describe it.

4. Have you ever vacationed at a beach? If so, where? Describe it.

5. Have you ever tried snorkeling or scuba diving? If so, where?
   Did you enjoy it?

6. Could the picture in the Dictionary be in your native country, or
   are there certain differences? Explain any differences.

4 Endless Stories

Read the following situations. Write a good ending using the
given words. It may take three or four sentences.

1. Nancy and her sister Olga came in from the water and couldn't
   find their things. They looked in all directions.

   beach umbrella   beach towel   beach chair   cooler

2. Betty was afraid of the water, and her friends were trying to
   convince her to go in.

   sand   wave   lifeguard   tube

3. Donald has been lifeguarding for several hours, and he is tired.
   The lifeguard who takes over from him is late.

   lifeguard chair   refreshment stand   binoculars

4. Two handsome young men see two beautiful young women at the beach.
   They want to meet them. They go up to them and begin to talk.

   Frisbee   beach ball   beach towel   cooler

116

67 Team Sports page 92
Ballfields page 93

1 Categories

On another sheet of paper, categorize all the words from page 92 as one of the following:

Clothing   Protective Gear   Field/Court Equipment

Tools to Hit With   Objects That Are Hit

2 Sports Broadcast

Read the following comments by sports broadcasters. Decide what game is being played. More than one answer may be possible.

1. The ball is now in our court. It hit the backboard! It's in ! _____ _____

2. She just spiked the ball over the net. It's a point! _____ _____ _____

3. The umpire is holding up his hands. It's a strike! _____ _____ _____

4. The goalie wasn't watching the ball. It's a goal! _____ _____ _____

5. The ball fell out of the outfielder's glove! It's a home run! _____ _____ ____

6. There's a penalty flag. He was holding Smith's face guard. ___ _____ _____ ____

7. It's a fight! He broke the stick while hitting number ten on the helmet. _____ _____

8. He hit the puck right past the sleeping goalie. _____ _____

9. He hit the ball so hard it broke the bat! _____

10. The ball hit the batter in the knee. It's a good thing we're not playing with a hard ball. _____

_____

3 Sporty Definitions

Read the following definitions. Decide which words from page 93 are being defined.

_____ 1. the person who makes the final decision in football

_____ 2. the place where the baseball pitcher stands

_____ 3. a football player who calls the signals and directs the offensive play

117

_____ 4. the place where the spectators sit

_____ 5. the football player to the right of the center and between the guard and the end

_____ 6. the shelter facing the baseball diamond where the waiting batters and other players sit

_____ 7. the place where the batter stands

_____ 8. the person who trains or instructs the players

4 Idioms

With a partner, use a larger dictionary to find out what the following idioms mean. Explain what they mean and use each one in a sentence.

1. right off the bat _____

_____

2. to make a hit _____

_____

3. right on base _____

_____

4. armchair quarterback _____

_____

5. get on the ball _____

_____

6. to go to bat for someone _____

_____

1 Word Scramble

Unscramble the following sentences on another sheet of paper.

1. balance gymnast fell The from the beam
2. into The went the bowling gutter ball
3. that golfer used hole a putter The for
4. hands reins jockey held in The his the
5. the boxer leave the referee told to The ring

2 Individual Sports and the Olympics

Read the following paragraphs. Underline all of the words from page 94 that you find. Then, on another sheet of paper, categorize the sports you find into those that are played with another person and those that aren't.

Men and women have participated in individual sports for thousands of years. In 770 B.C., the ancient Greeks organized running events every four years to honor the god Zeus. Over the next several hundred years other competitions, such as boxing, wrestling, and chariot racing, were added to the running events. These ancient Olympics were stopped in the fourth century A.D. by the Roman emperor Theodosius.

The modern Olympics started up again in 1896 in Athens, Greece, and, except for times of world war, has continued every four years in different cities since then. The first few modern Olympics continued track and field events, boxing, and wrestling, but chariot racing was no longer a part of the competition! In addition, sports like gymnastics and lawn tennis (later to become modern tennis) were included. Although popular individual sports like Ping-Pong, racquetball, bowling, golf, and handball have never joined the Olympic schedule, the first winter Olympics in 1924 added ice skating and cross-country skiing. Other sports have been included through the years. Horse racing, although similar to the ancient sport of chariot racing, is not a modern Olympic event. Whether part of the Olympics or not, individual sports competition has certainly remained popular!

3 Olympic Questions

Answer the following questions on another sheet of paper.

1. Which three sports were part of both the ancient and modern Olympics? Which two are listed in the Dictionary?

2. Why do you think skiing and ice skating were not part of the ancient Olympics?

3. What two sports were added to the first few modern Olympics?

4. What six sports were mentioned as not being a part of the Olympics?

69 Fields and Courses page 95

1 Matching

Match the following ads and sports.

A. tennis   B. golf   C. skiing   D. racing

_____ 1. Ride our modern lifts to the best slopes in the USA!
_____ 2. Leave your troubles at home and bring your clubs!
_____ 3. Well-lit courts for night games.
_____ 4. Watch the excitement from the starting gate to the finish line.
_____ 5. A difficult course with lovely fairways and greens.
_____ 6. Spend a day at the track!

2 Sporting Dialogues

Fill in the blanks in these dialogues with words from page 95.

1. A: I've never played _____ before.

   B: Just keep your eyes on the net and don't step over the _____ line.

2. A: I don't like to carry my _____ _____ all over the _____.

   B: Let's get a golf _____ next time.

3. A: The horses are in the final _____ and nearing the _____ line!

   B: My horse is in first place!

4. A: I'll meet you at the ski _____. I have to check my _____.

   B: OK, see you there.

5. A: Hurry up and _____ off!

   B: Don't rush me! I don't want my golf ball to go into a _____

   _____ again.

3 Popularity Contest

Of the four sports on page 95, which is the most popular in your native country? The least popular? Write two paragraphs—the first telling why one is popular and the second on why the other is unpopular.

120

70 Sports Verbs pages 96–97

1 Model Sentences

Write a sentence about each of the sports players below. Use one word from each of the three groups in each sentence. Use words like *with, to, at, in, over, across,* and *into* in your sentences. You may use a word more than once. Review pages **90–95** before you begin.

Watch the first baseman throw the baseball to the pitcher's mound.

Sports Players	Actions	Balls	Equipment and Places
1. first baseman	serve	basketball	bat
2. tennis player	catch	ping-pong ball	racket
3. soccer player	kick	soccer ball	net
4. basketball player	throw	tennis ball	green
5. hockey player	pass	football	goal
6. volleyball player	shoot	baseball	paddle
7. catcher	hit	puck	pitcher's mound
8. football player	bounce	volleyball	hockey stick
9. batter			foot
10. ping-pong player			court
			mitt
			end zone
			basket

2 Sports Test

Read the following questions and circle the best answer. Review pages **90–95** before you begin.

1. Kim is going to start the tennis match. She should

   a) kick the ball.   b) serve the ball.   c) shoot the ball.

2. There are basketball players from the other team all around Tom. He should

   a) surf.   b) fall.   c) catch.   d) pass.

3. The quarterback has the football, and there is no one around him. He should

   a) run with the ball.   b) bounce the ball.   c) hit the ball.

4. Beth has the ball and is close to her own team's basket. She should

   a) serve the ball.   b) shoot the ball.   c) hit the ball.   d) run with the ball.

5. The swimmer wants to be with the others in the pool. She should

   a) ride into the pool.   b) bounce into the pool.   c) dive into the pool.

3 Seasonal Sports

Write a four-paragraph article about seasonal sports in your native country. Write one paragraph on each season—summer, fall, winter, and spring. Tell which sports are played at each time and why. Use as many words from page **90–97** as possible. Read your essay to the class.

1 A Musical Survey

●
○○ Interview another student using the form below. Report your findings to the class.

Do you play a musical instrument? _____ If so, which one? _____

Have you ever taken music lessons? _____ If so, for how long? _____

  For what instrument? _____

Do any of your family members play a musical instrument? _____

  If so, who? _____ What does he/she play? _____

Who is your favorite musician? _____

What does he/she play? _____

2 Types of Musical Instruments

●
●○ Read the following essay and write the correct word after the definitions. There may be more than one good answer.

Musical instruments are usually classified by how they produce sound. For instance, musicians make sound on stringed instruments by hitting, plucking, or drawing a bow across tightly stretched strings. The piano is an example of the first method. Those instruments that are plucked can be plucked by the fingers, as with the harp, or with either the fingers or a pick, as with the guitar, ukelele, banjo, and mandolin. Bows are used on instruments like the violin, viola, cello, and the bass, although sometimes these can be plucked, too.

  In wind instruments, a vibrating column of air makes the sound. Sometimes the air is put into motion mechanically, as with the organ, but usually the musician blows into the instrument. The wind instruments can be further classified into woodwinds and brass. The woodwinds were originally made of wood, and most have reeds, which help to form the sound. The clarinet has a single reed, while the oboe and the bassoon have double reeds. The flute is an exception—it has no reed.

  The brass instruments were originally made of brass, and the musician's lips take the place of reeds. They all have mouthpieces. The French horn has a funnel-shaped mouthpiece, while the trombone, trumpet, and tuba have cup-shaped mouthpieces. The saxophone is the exception here because, although it has a mouthpiece, there is a reed in the mouthpiece.

Percussion instruments produce sounds when they are hit together or with a tool. They are made of wood, like the xylophone, or metal, like the cymbals, or tightly stretched skin, like the various types of drums. The tambourine is a combination of the last two types. It's interesting to see how many ways we can make musical sounds.

1. A stringed instrument played by hitting the strings _____

2. A stringed instrument played by either plucking or bowing _____

3. A wind instrument which is not blown into _____

4. A woodwind without a reed _____

5. A brass instrument with a reed _____

6. A percussion instrument made of metal and skin _____

3 Special Instruments

Can you think of a traditional instrument commonly played in your native country that is not commonly played in the United States? If so, write a short paragraph about it. Describe it, compare it to one of the instruments mentioned in the above reading, and tell what kind of music is usually played on it. Can you play this instrument?

72 Music, Dance, and Theater page 99

1 Categories

○●
○○
Put the words from page 99 into the following categories.

People   Parts of a Stage   Parts of a Theater   Equipment

2 Dictionary Work

●●
●○
Words often have more than one meaning. Read the definitions for these words and circle the one that relates to music, dance, and theater.

1. curtain
   a) a window drapery
   b) a screen separating the stage from the auditorium in a theater
   c) the closing scene of a play

2. stage
   a) a platform for a microscope on which the object to be examined is placed
   b) a horse-drawn passenger coach
   c) a step in the process of the development of something
   d) a raised platform for entertaining

3. program
   a) a short outline of the order of some entertainment
   b) a plan for a computer
   c) a performance in a theater

4. conductor
   a) a person who collects money on some means of public transportation
   b) a leader of a musical group
   c) a substance which transmits electricity, sound, or heat

5. usher
   a) a servant who has charge of a door or hall
   b) an officer who walks in front of an important person
   c) a person who escorts people to their seat

6. baton
   a) a stick with which a leader directs an orchestra
   b) a stick passed from one runner to another in a race
   c) a stick with a ball on the end used by a drum major in a band

7. podium
   a) a low wall serving as a foundation
   b) a raised platform for an orchestral conductor
   c) a raised platform for giving lectures

3 Personal Experience

●○
●●
Have you ever performed in front of a group of people? If so, explain what it was like. Use as many words from page 99 as possible, even if you have to mention what was <u>not</u> part of your experience!

73 Electronics and Photography page 100

1 Matching

●   It is necessary to have special equipment to do certain jobs.
○○   Match the jobs with the equipment.

_____ 1. Take a picture in a dark room.   a. calculator

_____ 2. Figure the cost of food for the week.   b. VCR

_____ 3. Show your latest vacation slides.   c. headphones

_____ 4. Watch a videocassette movie.   d. screen

_____ 5. Listen to music while others are sleeping.   e. flash

2 The Perfect Gift

●   The following people are about to have a birthday. Read about
●○   them and decide what you'd buy for them from the items on
page 100. There may be more than one good gift for each
person.

1. Paul has just become a father for the first time. _____

2. Sandy is a businesswoman who often needs to figure the costs of things at new prices. _____

_____

3. Ben is a salesman who makes lots of graphs and charts. _____

4. Diane is about to take a long trip. She has a new camera. _____

5. George is a jogger who easily gets bored. _____

6. Mark just bought a VCR. _____

7. Susie just bought a CD player. _____

8. Joan is a music lover who appreciates the very best sound. _____

3 Class Survey

●   As a class, decide which large piece of equipment is the most
●●   popular, which is least popular, and why. See if any class
members have more than one of any of the pieces of equipment
listed.

126

1 A Hard Job

● You have a job to do. Which tools and materials would you
○○ choose? You may use a word more than once.

1. Knit a sweater. _____

2. Sew on a button. _____

3. Put in a zipper. _____ _____

4. Shorten a dress. _____

5. Make a suit. __ _____

6. Make a quilt. ____ _____

2 Fill in the Blanks

● Fill in the blanks in each of the following sentences so that they
●○ will be sensible. There may be more than one correct answer.
Don't forget to use plurals if necessary.

1. While attaching the _____ _____ to her material, Fran stuck herself with a

   ____ _____.

2. The tailor measured the customer with a _____ __ _____ before he
   put the hem in his pants.

3. Mary had to choose the _____ before she knew how big to make the
   buttonholes.

4. Christie bought ten _____ of wool and some _____

   _____ before she began to knit her jacket.

5. She ran out of _____ and had to use the color closest to what she had.

6. She cut out her _____ with a _____ of _____ and
   then began to make the skirt.

7. There weren't any pins left in the _____, so she used a couple of

   ____ _____.

8. She always wears a _____ because her finger usually gets very sore from the

   __ _____.

9. The sewing teacher checked to see if her students' _____ were straight.

10. Her _____ _____ doesn't make buttonholes, so she had to do them by hand.

11. The beautiful _____ on the pillowcase was very colorful.

12. She didn't want the material to ravel, so she cut it with

_____ _____.

3 Your Hobby

What are the most popular handicrafts in your native country? Write a paragraph about these handicrafts—who does them, on what kind of material, and for what reason?

75 Prepositions of Description page 102
Prepositions of Motion page 103

1 Question and Answer Time

Ask a partner the whereabouts of the ten classroom nouns listed below. Try to use as many prepositions from page 102 as possible. After you're finished, do it as a class activity.

1. chalk
2. teacher's desk
3. your pencil
4. the students
5. clock

6. purse
7. bulletin board
8. chalkboard
9. tallest student
10. shortest student

2 The Lost Dog

Write any preposition from pages 102–103 in the following blanks. There may be more than one good answer, and you may use a preposition more than once.

Joe Adams was walking _____ _____ a friend's house when he saw his neighbor's dog

run _____ the street. Joe watched in horror as the dog ran _____ two

cars and then hid _____ a parked car. Joe had no idea how the dog had gotten

_____ _____ his owner. The dog was almost always

_____ the backyard _____ Joe's house, running _____

one side _____ the other. Joe tried to call the dog, but it wouldn't come

_____ him. Joe walked all _____ the parked car, calling the dog's

name. After a minute or so, the dog ran _____ the hill and _____ a

parking lot. Joe followed for a while, but then walked back _____ the hill and

_____ his neighbor's house to report the runaway dog. On the way, he met the

worried owner who said the dog had jumped _____ the backyard fence!

3 On Your Own

Look at the picture on pages **90–91**. Then, on another sheet of paper, describe the scene using as many prepositions from pages 102–103 as possible. Underline the prepositions as you use them.